I Remember,
I Remember

I Remember, I Remember

One Hundred Poems on Childhood

Edited by
A.D.P. Briggs

Illustrated by
Sophie Allport

ORION

AN ORION PAPERBACK

First published in Great Britain in 2005 by Orion,
an imprint of Orion Books Ltd,
Orion House, 5 Upper St Martin's Lane, London WC2H 9EA

10 9 8 7 6 5 4 3 2 1

Introduction and selection © Orion Paperbacks, 2005
Illustrations copyright © Sophie Allport, 2005

A CIP catalogue record for this book
is available from the British Library.

ISBN 0 75381 866 3

Printed and bound in Italy.

www.orionbooks.co.uk

～ Contents

∼ *Introduction*

Childhood has no forebodings, but then it is soothed by no memories of outlived sorrow.   George Eliot

The Lost World of Childhood

We are all experts on the world of childhood. We have been there, come through and emerged on the other side. Now that we have put away childish things we can look back on that curious world, knowing what it was all about. Or can we? Looking back is a strange experience. Was it a time of lost innocence and happiness, or an age of fear and frustration? Happy days, or a process of increasing anxiety and pain as we collided with a reality less loving than mother's arms had promised?

Childhood is not simple. It is not even logical. Some children born into squalor seem to have sailed through their early years, while others issued with silver spoons have suffered miserably. Nor can Milton be relied on when he tells us that 'The childhood shows the man/ As morning shows the day.' This is an epigram; more wit than wisdom. Do we not know imposing adults who have grown from dull children, rogues from innocents, and reformed characters from bad lots? Childhood turns out to be no more susceptible to generalisation than life as a whole.

Given this instability, it is not surprising to discover more diversity and contradiction than uniformity in our poetic heritage of poems on childhood. For one thing, our poets vary in their taste for the topic. You won't find all that much about childhood in Shakespeare, Byron or Keats. By contrast, there are poets who cannot leave it alone: Wordsworth, Blake, Longfellow, Swinburne, Robert Louis Stevenson. Also Winthrop Mackworth Praed … Winthrop Mackworth who?

Lightweights and Heavyweights

Praed was a short-lived poetaster of the early nineteenth century who might have been forgotten but for the popularity of his appealing verses about children, fortuitously preserved by the Victorians in collections. (See 'Childhood and His Visitors', with its clever idea of presenting a little boy who is too busy enjoying himself to listen to Time, Guilt, Sorrow, the Muse or Wisdom when they call). This is a province which has welcomed many a minor poet who happens to have struck a memorable note on the sentimental subject of childhood. Bloomfield, Philips, Locker-Lampson and Beeching have provided enjoyable examples for this volume. So does Ethel Lynn Beers, whose famous poem 'Which Shall it Be?', a tale of parents trying to choose one of their seven children for virtual sale to a rich couple, is widely accepted as a masterpiece of Victorian sentimental writing, though most people would struggle to name another work by her.

Poems like these, more entertainment than art or wisdom, deserve their continuing life in anthologies. Anyone thirsting for quality, however, should turn to Walt Whitman, whose poem, 'There was a child went forth …', is a truly complex and rewarding childhood poem. The boy sallies forth newly born each morning, avidly assimilating all the good things of his immediate world: the all things bright and beautiful of flowers, birdsong, baby animals, fish, plants and fruit. He starts to look deeper, and notices contrasts: comic and serious people, girls and boys, black and white, some people friendly, some quarrelsome. He sees that the essence of life is change rather than certainty. His parents are starkly presented: woman and man, affectionate and distant, gentle and gruff. Doubt begins to strike, and the world shocks the boy with its indeterminate character. His vision, having deepened, now broadens through an awareness of buildings, traffic, ships, the ocean. In thirty-nine long lines of rolling verse he leads us through the creation, preservation and development of human life. It is an optimistic vision, dwelling on vitality and potential rather than pain or morbidity, though the dark uncertainty introduced in mid-poem, temporarily suppressed, seems likely to return:

> The doubts of day-time and the doubts of the night-time,
> the curious whether and how…

Death, which stands beyond a child's comprehension, is never mentioned. The luscious complexity and enchantment of our world will come alive again to every reader of this poem, with a new look of pristine sharpness shining in the eyes of a boy. His awareness is acquired gradually; a contrasting vision of childhood suddenly exploding into puberty is presented by Carol Ann Duffy in a poem with a devastating last line 'In Mrs Tilscher's Class'.

Blest Hours of Infantine Content

Walt Whitman's positive angle on childhood is adopted by many writers on the subject, perhaps the majority. George Eliot looks back on happy times spent with her idolised older brother, whom she seems to have followed around like a puppy, showing little of the forthrightness soon to dawn in her writing, her characters and her personal relations with men. She sums up the experience as coming 'From those blest hours of infantine content' ('Brother and Sister' (2)). Beeching's little boy finds exhilaration on two wheels in 'Going Down Hill on a Bicycle'. James Hogg shows us another little boy out at play in the hayfields ('A Boy's Song'). Philips's baby girl reminds the poet of a happy little bird as she chirps forth her 'petty joys' and he refers to her condition as 'This thy present happy lot' ('To Miss Charlotte Pulteney in Her Mother's Arms'). Stevenson's youngster turns his sick-bed into a battlefield and then a whole country set among the rolling hills of his eiderdown in 'The Land of Counterpane'. Edward Thomas shows us a child in an orchard noticing the world and eager to learn about it; enraptured and excited he cries out,

There are millions of things for me to learn.

John Betjeman, recalling his childhood days in affectionate detail, also remembers the boyish thrill of turning over stones to see what comes out; his wonderment delays him, and invokes punishment – fortunately he has a good friend, his bear, to turn to for consolation. Ted Hughes captures his little daughter's amazement at the beauty of nature much more succinctly in 'Full Moon and Little Frieda'.

Thomas Hood recalls a time when his 'spirit flew in feathers', and summer pools could hardly cool the fever on his brow, and in the last lines of the poem 'I remember, I remember' he claims that those early days with their childish ignorance saw him nearer to heaven than he can ever be again. This theme is a favourite one of Wordsworth's. For him babyhood and childhood sound the last faint echoes of a fuller existence which human consciousness has proceeded from and shall return to:

> But trailing clouds of glory do we come
>   From God, who is our home:
> Heaven lies about us in our infancy!
> Shades of the prison-house begin to close
>   Upon the growing Boy...

These inspiring Wordsworthian ideas, set in such splendid verses, established a standard well beyond the reach of many a nineteenth-century religious poet moved by the sight of a tiny baby or happy little girl. We have chosen not to fill out this collection with sentimental religious pieces of that kind from the Victorian era, though there are hundreds to go at. Poems with titles like 'The Minister's Daughter', 'Dot Baby Off Mine' and 'Poor Little Joe' have been left in their deserved and gathering obscurity. Almost alone amongst his contemporaries, Swinburne strikes a less obviously plangent note when treating this theme. Poems of his like 'Of Such is the Kingdom of Heaven' and 'A Child's Laughter' keep things simple and can still move the reader, though they too are a long way short of Wordsworth's towering genius in this area.

The Wiping of Noses
It is often the steady hand of realism that rescues a childhood poem from maudlin or tearful excess. Thomas Hood, for instance, loves his infant son, John, like a good father, calling him a 'happy elf', a 'tricksy puck' and a 'cherub of earth' in the opening lines of the first three stanzas of 'A Parental Ode to My Son, Aged Three Years and Five Months'. These coy epithets, which would spell

ruination if left to survive and prosper, are there to be shot down, and the poet picks them off one by one. All through the poem he sets up one fine fatherly phrase after another, deliberately following each one with a bracketed aside that brings lofty fantasy down to earth. The poem is a triumph of bathos. In the open text the child is doted upon adoringly; in brackets he sheds tears, pokes peas in his ears, swallows a pin, spills ink, falls down, squints, makes himself sick – or comes very near to doing all these things and much more. The last stanza brings the technique to fulfilment, beginning

> Thou pretty opening rose!
> (Go to your mother, child, and wipe your nose!)

Nowadays, of course, the child would have had to do this last job himself, but for his time Hood is being admirably modern in his debunking of excessive sentiment.

There are other ways of undermining the over-emotional appeal of childhood. De Vere shows us laughing children playing in a school-yard but turns attention away from them to the surrounding world of dire depravity ('A Convent School in a Corrupt City'). In 'Feigned Courage' Mary Lamb depicts a bold young hero, the scourge of all villains and enemies, who cries when he hurts his hand:

> Achilles weeps, great Hector hangs his head!
> And the Black Prince goes whimpering to bed.

John Clare plays with our expectations by seeming to evoke sledges and snowballs in a poem with a pretty title, 'Schoolboys in Winter', but his children move with a slow step and play halfheartedly – it turns out they are creeping like snail unwillingly to school. A similar sentiment runs through Blake's poem, 'The School Boy'. Here is a poet who truly knows how to temper a sense of beauty with an accompanying feeling of dread. His 'Songs of Innocence' (1789) were followed by 'Songs of Experience' (1794); both contain several poems about childhood and his 'Infant Joy' lasts only a while before it is neutralised by 'Infant Sorrow'.

The Tyranny of Age

Speaking of sorrow, we are faced with one category of childhood poems that must be confronted, however unpleasant this may be. These are works in which nasty things that ought not to happen to anyone are seen affecting the most vulnerable amongst us, our children.

First, the question of premature death. The commonest of all childhood poems, in the nineteenth century at least, are those which mourn the passing of a baby or infant. They serve as a salutary reminder of our own good fortune to be born in an age where few children die. This volume could have been filled with them, most with deeply religious overtones, but instead of letting the subject run riot (for most of these works take the lachrymose stories beyond acceptance by the third-millennium palate) we have left it to a much earlier writer to tell a poignant story that may be taken to stand for many others. Ben Jonson wrote two poems with similar titles, 'On My First Daughter' and 'On My First Son'. The former lived only for six months, the latter for seven years, and Ben and his wife had no more children. The first poem begins 'Here lies...', and the second, 'Farewell, thou child ...'; both are harrowing accounts of a cruel occurrence. After this the outpourings of later poets, all too understandable in themselves, can sometimes seem to cloy. Christina Rossetti will be one of the few who can catch the beauty of a dead child and see something obliquely positive in this ultimate experience ('Buds and Babies'). Seamus Heaney avoids excess by recalling his young brother's death through his own eyes as a child; the smallness of the dead body and his little life is poignantly borne out by the coffin, 'A four foot box, a foot for every year.'

It is not only death that leaves a dark stain on childhood. All too often deprivation and cruelty also play their part. For every poem of joy there is one of sorrow. In 'The Street Children's Dance' Mathilde Blind offers a bleak picture of underprivileged city children taken out of themselves, momentarily touched by glory on an April afternoon but doomed to relapse into brutish poverty.

Similar in tone is Blake's moving tale of 'The Chimney Sweeper'. Sickness and the fear of death haunt other poets. The full range of childish misery is played out by Elizabeth Barrett Browning in 'The Cry of the Children', perhaps to excess – we have included only the first five sections of a much longer poem.

For the very darkest piece in this collection we turn to a narrative by George Crabbe made famous in our age as the libretto for an opera by Benjamin Britten, the story of Peter Grimes. This tragic tale, from which we offer only a brief couple of sections, hands down violence from one generation to the next. Peter's ghastly father ensures that his son will be even more vicious and violent than he has been. The son who once fulminated against 'the tyranny of age' will push his own cruelty to children through flogging and every kind of abuse right on to nothing less than serial murder.

And in amongst these dark satanic poems there are others which, although lighter in tone, bear down upon children with strong warnings from adulthood. Walter Savage Landor solemnly enjoins his serious son to emulate the saint whose picture he admires ('Before a Saint's Picture'). Thomas Moore warns a young friend not to waste too much time being idle or joyful when there are heaven and virtue to think about ('To a Boy'), while the dour Scot, Alexander Smart, counsels all little boys against doing anything by day that they may come to regret by nightfall ('The Truant'). Ann and Jane Taylor place a heavy burden of gratitude on any small person lucky enough to have been smiled on by goodness and grace sufficiently to become 'A happy English child' ('A Child's Hymn of Praise'). Even the well-meant poem by James Ballantyne which opens our collection seems heavy-handed in its cautious advice to an exploring baby: 'Creep Afore Ye Gang'. As we read these amusingly outdated pieces now, we shudder for any miserable child to whom they may have been read for serious instruction. A more successful way of persuading the young to behave nobly is through emotion, example and inspiration; Henry Newbolt's famous poem about the end of a cricket match, 'There's a breathless hush in the Close tonight ...', reminds us of a long-gone age when the principles of fair play, courage and self-sacrifice came into every boy's programme of education.

To end on a sweeter note, let us celebrate the opportunity to issue again one or two longer poems (or extracts from narrative poems) which deal with children, were once enjoyed and learned by children, but were also absorbed with much pleasure by parents and teachers. Exciting poems like 'The Wreck of the Hesperus', 'Hiawatha', 'Sweet and Low', and 'Casabianca' ('The Boy Stood on the Burning Deck') still deserve to be read aloud, learned by heart and declaimed to others. Dare we hope that schools and parents will one day work together to restore a tradition that seems to have been eroded? Childhood is the time for poetry and poems about children and childhood are a good subject to begin with.

A. D. P. BRIGGS

I Remember,
I Remember

Creep Afore Ye Gang

Creep awa', my bairnie, creep afore ye gang,
Cock ye baith your lugs to your auld Granny's sang;
Gin ye gang as far ye will think the road lang—
Creep awa', my bairnie, creep afore ye gang.

Creep awa', my bairnie, ye're ower young to learn
To tot up and down yet, my bonnie wee bairn;
Better creeping cannie, than fa'ing wi' a bang,
Duntin' a' your wee brow – creep afore ye gang.

Ye'll creep, an' ye'll laugh, an' ye'll nod to your mother,
Watching ilka step o' your wee dowsy brother;
Rest ye on the floor till your wee limbs grow strang,
And ye'll be a braw chield yet – creep afore ye gang.

The wee birdie fa's when it tries ower soon to flee;
Folks are sure to tumble when they climb ower hie;
They wha dinna walk aright are sure to come to wrang—
Creep awa', my bairnie, creep afore ye gang.

Going Down Hill on a Bicycle: A Boy's Song

With lifted feet, hands still,
I am poised, and down the hill
Dart, with heedful mind;
The air goes by in a wind.

Swifter and yet more swift,
Till the heart with a mighty lift
Makes the lungs laugh, the throat cry:—
'O bird, see; see, bird, I fly.

'Is this, is this your joy?
O bird, then I, though a boy,
For a golden moment share
Your feathery life in air!'

Say, heart, is there aught like this
In a world that is full of bliss?
'Tis more than skating, bound
Steel-shod to the level ground.

Speed slackens now, I float
Awhile in my airy boat;
Till, when the wheels scarce crawl,
My feet to the treadles fall.

Alas, that the longest hill
Must end in a vale; but still,
Who climbs with toil, wheresoe'er,
Shall find wings waiting there.

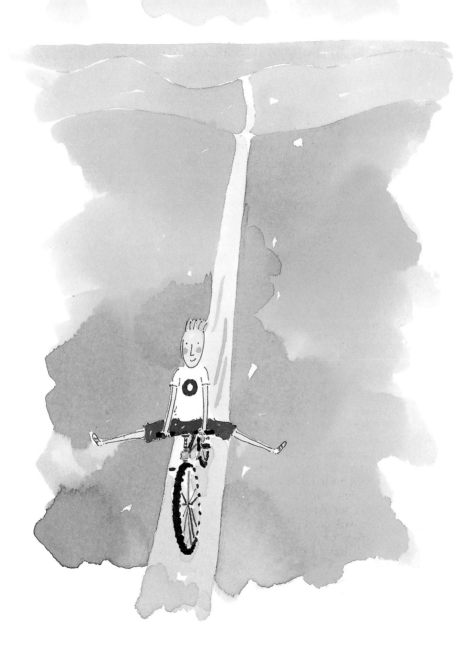

Which Shall It Be?

'Which shall it be? Which shall it be?'
I look'd at John – John look'd at me
(Dear, patient John, who loves me yet
As well as though my locks were jet);
And when I found that I must speak,
My voice seemed strangely low and weak:
'Tell me again what Robert said.'
And then I, listening, bent my head.
'This is his letter: "I will give
A house and land while you shall live,
If, in return, from out your seven,
One child to me for aye is given."'
I looked at John's old garments worn,
I thought of all that John had borne
Of poverty and work and care,
Which I, though willing, could not share;
I thought of seven mouths to feed,
Of seven little children's need,
And then of this. 'Come, John,' said I,
'We'll choose among them as they lie
Asleep;' so, walking hand in hand,
Dear John and I surveyed our band.
First to the cradle lightly stepped,
Where the new nameless baby slept.
'Shall it be Baby?' whispered John.
I took his hand, and hurried on
To Lily's crib. Her sleeping grasp
Held her old doll within its clasp;
Her dark curls lay like gold alight,
A glory 'gainst the pillow white.
Softly her father stoop'd to lay
His rough hand down in loving way.
When dream or whisper made her stir,
Then huskily said John, 'Not her, not her!'
We stopp'd beside the trundle bed,

And one long ray of lamplight shed
Athwart the boyish faces there,
In sleep so pitiful and fair;
I saw on Jamie's rough, red cheek
A tear undried. Ere John could speak,
'He's but a baby, too,' said I,
And kiss'd him as we hurried by.
Pale, patient Robbie's angel face
Still in his sleep bore suffering's trace.
'No, for a thousand crowns, not him!'
We whisper'd, while our eyes were dim.
Poor Dick! bad Dick! our wayward son,
Turbulent, reckless, idle one—
Could he be spared? Nay; He who gave
Bids us befriend him to his grave:
Only a mother's heart can be
Patient enough for such as he;
'And so,' said John, 'I would not dare
To send him from her bedside prayer.'
Then stole we softly up above
And knelt by Mary, child of love.
'Perhaps for her 'twould better be,'
I said to John. Quite silently
He lifted up a curl astray
Across her cheek in wilful way,
And shook his head: 'Nay, love: not thee.'
The while my heart beat audibly.
Only one more, our eldest lad,
Trusty and truthful, good and glad—
So like his father. 'No, John, no—
I cannot, will not, let him go.'
And so we wrote, in courteous way.
We could not give one child away;
And afterward toil lighter seemed,
Thinking of that of which we dreamed.
Happy in truth that not one face
We missed from its accustomed place;
Thankful to work for all the seven,
Trusting the rest to One in heaven.

On the Gift of a Book to a Child

Child! do not throw this book about!
  Refrain from the unholy pleasure
Of cutting all the pictures out!
  Preserve it as your chiefest treasure.

Child, have you never heard it said
  That you are heir to all the ages?
Why, then, your hands were never made
  To tear these beautiful thick pages!

Your little hands were made to take
  The better things and leave the worse ones:
They also may be used to shake
  The Massive Paws of Elder Persons.

And when your prayers complete the day,
  Darling, your little tiny hands
Were also made, I think, to pray
  For men that lose their fairylands.

from *'Summoned by Bells', Chapter 1, 'Before MCMXIV'*

Safe were those evenings of the pre-war world
When firelight shone on green linoleum;
I heard the church bells hollowing out the sky,
Deep beyond deep, like never-ending stars,
And turned to Archibald, my safe old bear,
Whose woollen eyes looked sad or glad at me,
Whose ample forehead I could wet with tears,
Whose half-moon ears received my confidence,
Who made me laugh, who never let me down.
I used to wait for hours to see him move,
Convinced that he could breathe. One dreadful day
They hid him from me as a punishment:
Sometimes the desolation of that loss
Comes back to me and I must go upstairs
To see him in the sawdust, so to speak,
Safe and returned to his idolator ...

The sunlit weeks between were full of maids:
Sarah, with orange wig and horsy teeth,
Was so bad-tempered that she scarcely spoke;
Maud was my hateful nurse who smelt of soap
And forced me to eat chewy bits of fish,
Thrusting me back to babyhood with threats
Of nappies, dummies and the feeding bottle.
She rubbed my face in messes I had made
And was the first to tell me about Hell,
Admitting she was going there herself.
Sometimes, thank God, they left me all alone
In our small patch of garden in the front,
With clinker rockery and London Pride
And barren lawn and lumps of yellow clay

As mouldable as smelly Plasticine.
I used to turn the heavy stones to watch
The shiny red and waiting centipede
Which darted out of sight; the woodlouse slow
And flat; the other greyish-bluey kind
Which rolled into a ball till I was gone
Out of the gate to venture down the hill.
    'You're late for dinner, John.' I feel again
That awful feeling, fear confused with thrill,
As I would be unbuttoned, bent across
Her starchy apron, screaming 'Don't – Maud – don't!'
Till dissolution, bed and kindly fur
Of agéd, uncomplaining Archibald.

Infant Joy

'I have no name;
I am but two days old.'
What shall I call thee?
'I happy am,
Joy is my name.'
Sweet joy befall thee!

Pretty joy!
Sweet joy but two days old,
Sweet joy I call thee:
Thou dost smile,
I sing the while,
Sweet joy befall thee.

Infant Sorrow

My mother groan'd, my father wept;
Into the dangerous world I leapt,
Helpless, naked, piping loud,
Like a fiend hid in a cloud.

Struggling in my father's hands,
Striving against my swadling bands,
Bound and weary, I thought best
To sulk upon my mother's breast.

The School Boy

I love to rise in a summer morn,
When the birds sing on every tree;
The distant huntsman winds his horn,
And the sky-lark sings with me.
O! What sweet company.

But to go to school in a summer morn,
O! it drives all joy away;
Under a cruel eye outworn
The little ones spend the day
In sighing and dismay.

Ah! then at times I drooping sit,
And spend many an anxious hour;
Nor in my book can I take delight,
Nor sit in learning's bower,
Worn thro' with the dreary shower.

How can the bird that is born for joy
Sit in a cage and sing?
How can a child when fears annoy
But droop his tender wing,
And forget his youthful spring?

O! father & mother, if buds are nip'd
And blossoms blown away,
And if the tender plants are strip'd
Of their joy in the springing day
By sorrow and care's dismay,

How shall the summer arise in joy,
Or the summer fruits appear?
Or how shall we gather what griefs destroy,
Or bless the mellowing year
When the blasts of winter appear?

The Chimney Sweeper

When my mother died I was very young,
And my father sold me while yet my tongue
Could scarcely cry "'weep! 'weep! 'weep! 'weep!'
So your chimneys I sweep, & in soot I sleep.

There's little Tom Dacre, who cried when his head,
That curl'd like a lamb's back, was shav'd; so I said,
'Hush, Tom, never mind it, for when your head's bare,
You know that the soot cannot spoil your white hair.'

And so he was quiet, & that very night,
As Tom was asleeping he had such a sight:
That thousands of sweepers, Dick, Joe, Ned & Jack,
Were all of them lock'd up in coffins of black;

And by came an Angel who had a bright key,
And he open'd the coffins & set them all free;
Then down a green plain leaping, laughing they run,
And wash in a river and shine in the Sun.

Then naked & white, all their bags left behind,
They rise upon clouds, and sport in the wind;
And the Angel told Tom, if he'd be a good boy,
He'd have God for his father & never want joy.

And so Tom awoke; and we rose in the dark,
And got with our bags & our brushes to work.
Tho' the morning was cold, Tom was happy & warm;
So if all do their duty, they need not fear harm.

The Ecchoing Green

The Sun does arise,
And make happy the skies;
The merry bells ring
To welcome the Spring;
The sky-lark and thrush,
The birds of the bush,
Sing louder around
To the bells' chearful sound,
While our sports shall be seen
On the Ecchoing Green.

Old John with white hair
Does laugh away care,
Sitting under the oak
Among the old folk.
They laugh at our play,
And soon they all say:
'Such, such were the joys
When we all, girls & boys,
In our youth-time were seen
On the Ecchoing Green.'

Till the little ones weary
No more can be merry;
The sun does descend,
And our sports have an end.
Round the laps of their mothers
Many sisters and brothers,
Like birds in their nest,
Are ready for rest;
And sport no more seen
On the darkening Green.

from *The Street Children's Dance*

Now the earth in fields and hills
Stirs with pulses of the Spring,
Nest-embowering hedges ring
With interminable trills;
Sunlight runs a race with rain,
All the world grows young again.

Young as at the hour of birth:
From the grass the daisies rise
With the dew upon their eyes,
Sun-awakened eyes of earth;
Fields are set with cups of gold;
Can this budding world grow old?..

Can this earth run o'er with beauty,
Laugh through leaf and flower and grain,
While in close-pent court and lane,
In the air so thick and sooty,
Little ones pace to and fro,
Weighted with their parent's woe?

Woe-predestined little ones!
Putting forth their buds of life
In an atmosphere of strife,
And crime-breeding ignorance;
Where the bitter surge of care
Freezes to a dull despair.

Dull despair and misery
Lies about them from their birth;
Ugly curses, uglier mirth,
Are their earliest lullaby;
Fathers have they without name,
Mothers crushed by want and shame.

Brutish, overburdened mothers,
With their hungry children cast
Half-nude to the nipping blast;
Little sisters with their brothers
Dragging in their arms all day
Children nigh as big as they.

Children withered by the street:
Shouting, flouting, roaring after
Passers-by with gibes and laughter,
Diving between horses' feet,
In and out of drays and barrows,
Recklessly, like London sparrows ...

Blossoms of humanity!
Poor soiled blossoms in the dust!
Through the thick defiling crust
Of soul-stifling poverty,
In your features may be traced
Children's beauty half effaced—

Childhood, stunted in the shadow
Of the light-debarring walls:
Not for you the cuckoo calls
O'er the silver-threaded meadow;
Not for you the lark on high
Pours his music from the sky.

Ah! you have your music too!
And come flocking round that player
Grinding at his organ there,
Summer-eyed and swart of hue,
Rattling off his well-worn tune
On this April afternoon.

Lovely April lights of pleasure,
Flit o'er want-beclouded features
Of those little outcast creatures,
As they swing with rhythmic measure,
In the courage of their rags,
Lightly o'er the slippery flags.

Little footfalls, lightly glancing
In a luxury of motion,
Supple as the waves of ocean,
In your elemental dancing,
How you fly, and wheel, and spin,
For your hearts too dance within!

Dance along with mirth and laughter,
Buoyant, fearless and elate,
Dancing in the teeth of fate,
Ignorant of your hereafter,
That with all its tragic glooms
Blinding on your future looms.

Past and future, hence away!
Joy, diffused throughout all the earth,
Centre in this moment's mirth
Of ecstatic holiday:
Once in all their live's dark story
Touch them, Fate! with April glory!

The Blind Child

Where's the blind child, so admirably fair,
With guileless dimples, and with flaxen hair
That waves in every breeze? He's often seen
Beside yon cottage wall, or on the green,
With others match'd in spirit and in size,
Health on their cheeks, and rapture in their eyes.
That full expanse of voice, to childhood dear,
Soul of their sports, is duly cherish'd here:
And hark! that laugh is his, that jovial cry;
He hears the ball and trundling hoop brush by,
And runs the giddy course with all his might,
A very child in everything but sight;
With circumscribed, but not abated powers—
Play, the great object of his infant hours!
In many a game he takes a noisy part,
And shows the native gladness of his heart;
But soon he hears, on pleasure all intent,
The new suggestion and the quick assent;

The grove invites, delight fills every breast—
To leap the ditch, and seek the downy nest.
Away they start; leave balls and hoops behind,
And one companion leave – the boy is blind!
His fancy paints their distant paths so gay,
That childish fortitude awhile gives way:
He feels the dreadful loss; yet short the pain,
Soon he resumes his cheerfulness again,
Pondering how best his moments to employ,
He sings his little songs of nameless joy;
Creeps on the warm green turf for many an hour,
And plucks by chance the white and yellow flower;
Soothing their stems while resting on his knees,
He binds a nosegay which he never sees;
Along the homeward path then feels his way,
Lifting his brow against the shining day,
And with a playful rapture round his eyes,
Presents a sighing parent with the prize.

Upon My Son Samuel his Going for England, Novem. 6, 1657

Thou mighty God of sea and land,
I here resign into thy hand
The son of prayers, of vows, of tears,
The child I stay'd for many years.
Thou heard'st me then, and gav'st him me;
Hear me again, I give him thee.
He's mine, but more, O Lord, thine own,
For sure thy grace on him is shown.
No friend I have like thee to trust,
For mortal helps are brittle dust.
Preserve, O Lord, from storms and wrack,
Protect him there, and bring him back;
And if thou shalt spare me a space,
That I again may see his face,
Then shall I celebrate thy praise,
And bless thee for't even all my days.
If otherwise I go to rest,
Thy will be done, for that is best;
Persuade my heart I shall him see
For ever happefy'd with thee.

'Come hither, child – who gifted thee'

'Come hither, child – who gifted thee
With power to touch that string so well?
How darest thou rouse up thoughts in me,
Thoughts that I would, but cannot quell?'

'Nay, chide not, lady; long ago
I heard those notes in Ula's hall;
And, had I known they'd waken woe
I'd weep, their music to recall.

'But thus it was: one festal night
When I was hardly six years old,
I stole away from crowds and light
And sought a chamber dark and cold.

'I had no one to love me there;
I knew no comrade and no friend;
And so I went to sorrow where
Heaven, only heaven, saw me bend.

'Loud blew the wind; 'twas sad to stay,
From all that splendour barred away.
I imaged in the lonely room
A thousand forms of fearful gloom;

'And, with my wet eyes raised on high,
I prayed to God that I might die.
Suddenly, in that silence drear,
A sound of music reached my ear;

'And then a note; I hear it yet,
So full of soul, so deeply sweet,
I thought that Gabriel's self had come
To take me to my father's home.

'Three times it rose, that seraph-strain,
Then died, nor lived ever again;
But still the words and still the tone
Swell round my heart when all alone.'

from *The Cry of the Children*

Do ye hear the children weeping, O my brothers,
Ere the sorrow comes with years?
They are leaning their young heads against their mothers,
And *that* cannot stop their tears.
The young lambs are bleating in the meadows,
The young birds are chirping in the nest,
The young fawns are playing with the shadows,
The young flowers are blowing toward the west—
But the young, young children, O my brothers,
They are weeping bitterly!
They are weeping in the playtime of the others,
In the country of the free.

Do you question the young children in the sorrow,
Why their tears are falling so?
The old man may weep for his to-morrow
Which is lost in Long ago.
The old tree is leafless in the forest,
The old year is ending in the frost,
The old wound, if stricken, is the sorest,
The old hope is hardest to be lost.
But the young, young children, O my brothers,
Do you ask them why they stand
Weeping sore before the bosoms of their mothers,
In our happy Fatherland?

They look up with their pale and sunken faces,
And their looks are sad to see,
For the man's hoary anguish draws and presses
Down the cheeks of infancy.
'Your old earth,' they say, 'is very dreary;
Our young feet,' they say, 'are very weak!
Few paces have we taken, yet are weary—

Our grave-rest is very far to seek.
Ask the aged why they weep, and not the children;
For the outside earth is cold;
And we young ones stand without, in our bewildering,
And the graves are for the old.'

'True,' say the children, 'it may happen
That we die before our time.
Little Alice died last year – her grave is shapen
Like a snowball, in the rime.
We lookcd into the pit prepared to take her.
Was no room for any work in the close clay!
From the sleep wherein she lieth none will wake her,
Crying, "Get up, little Alice, it is day."
If you listen by that grave, in sun and shower,
With your ear down, little Alice never cries.
Could we see her face, be sure we should not know her,
For the smile has time for growing in her eyes.
And merry go her moments, lulled and stilled in
The shroud by the kirk-chime!
'It is good when it happens,' say the children,
'That we die before our time.'

Alas, alas, the children! they are seeking
Death in life, as best to have.
They are binding up their hearts away from breaking,
With a cerement from a grave.
Go out, children, from the mine and from the city,
Sing out, children, as the little thrushes do.
Pluck your handfuls of the meadow-cowslips pretty,
Laugh aloud, to feel your fingers let them through!
But they answer, are your cowslips of the meadows
Like our weeds a-near the mine?
Leave us quiet in the dark of the coal-shadows,
From your pleasures fair and fine! . .

from '*The Pied Piper of Hamelin*'

The Piper, having rid Hamelin of its rats and been refused his fee, takes his revenge

XII

Once more he stept into the street
  And to his lips again
  Laid his long pipe of smooth straight cane;
And ere he blew three notes (such sweet
Soft notes as yet musician's cunning
  Never gave the enraptured air)
There was a rustling that seemed like a bustling
Of merry crowds justling at pitching and hustling,
Small feet were pattering, wooden shoes clattering,
Little hands clapping and little tongues chattering,
And, like fowls in a farm-yard when barley is scattering,
Out came the children running.
All the little boys and girls,
With rosy cheeks and flaxen curls,
And sparkling eyes and teeth like pearls,
Tripping and skipping, ran merrily after
The wonderful music with shouting and laughter.

XIII

The Mayor was dumb, and the Council stood
As if they were changed into blocks of wood,
Unable to move a step, or cry
To the children merrily skipping by,
—Could only follow with the eye
That joyous crowd at the Piper's back.
But how the Mayor was on the rack,
And the wretched Council's bosoms beat,
As the Piper turned from the High Street
To where the Weser rolled its waters
Right in the way of their sons and daughters!
However he turned from South to West,
And to Koppelberg Hill his steps addressed,
And after him the children pressed;
Great was the joy in every breast.
'He never can cross that mighty top!
'He's forced to let the piping drop,
'And we shall see our children stop!'
When, lo, as they reached the mountainside,
A wondrous portal opened wide,
As if a cavern was suddenly hollowed;
And the Piper advanced and the children followed,
And when all were in to the very last,
The door in the mountain-side shut fast.

A Poet's Welcome to his Love-Begotten Daughter; The First Instance that Entitled him to The Venerable Appellation of Father

Thou's welcome, wean! Mischanter fa' me,
If thoughts o' thee, or yet thy Mamie,
Shall ever daunton me or awe me,
   My bonie lady;
Or if I blush when thou shalt ca' me
   Tyta, or Daddie.

Though now they ca' me fornicator,
And tease my name in kintra clatter,
The mair they talk, I'm kend the better;
   E'en let them clash!
An auld wife's tongue's a feckless matter
   To gie ane fash.

Welcome! My bonie, sweet, wee dochter!
Though ye come here a wee unsought for;
And though your comin I hae fought for,
   Baith Kirk and Queir;
Yet by my faith, ye're no unwrought for,
   That I shall swear!

Wee image o' my bonie Betty,
As fatherly I kiss and daut thee,
As dear and near my heart I set thee,
   Wi' as gude will,
As a' the Priests had seen me get thee
   That's out o' h—.

Sweet fruit o' monie a merry dint,
My funny toil is no a' tint;
Though ye come to the warld asklent,
       Which fools may scoff at,
In my last plack your part's be in't,
       The better half o't.

Though I should be the waur bestead,
Thou's be as braw and bienly clad,
And thy young years as nicely bred
       Wi' education,
As any brat o' Wedlock's bed,
       In a' thy station.

Lord grant that thou may ay inherit
Thy Mither's looks an' gracefu' merit;
An' thy poor, worthless Daddie's spirit,
       Without his failins!
'Twad please me mair to see thee heir it
       Than stocked mailins!

For if thou be, what I wad hae thee,
And tak the counsel I shall gie thee,
I'll never rue my trouble wi' thee,
       The cost nor shame o't,
But be a loving Father to thee,
       And brag the name o't.

On The Birth of John William Rizzo Hoppner

His father's sense, his mother's grace,
   In him, I hope, will always fit so;
With – still to keep him in good case—
   The health and appetite of Rizzo.

Who?

Who is that child I see wandering, wandering
Down by the side of the quivering stream?
Why does he seem not to hear, though I call to him?
Where does he come from, and what is his name?

Why do I see him at sunrise and sunset
Taking, in old-fashioned clothes, the same track?
Why, when he walks, does he cast not a shadow
Though the sun rises and falls at his back?

Why does the dust lie so thick on the hedgerow
By the great field where a horse pulls the plough?
Why do I see only meadows, where houses
Stand in a line by the riverside now?

Why does he move like a wraith by the water,
Soft as the thistledown on the breeze blown?
When I draw near him so that I may hear him,
Why does he say that his name is my own?

Schoolboys in Winter

The schoolboys still their morning rambles take
To neighbouring village school with playing speed,
Loitering with pastime's leisure till they quake,
Oft looking up the wild-geese droves to heed,
Watching the letters which their journeys make;
Or plucking haws on which the fieldfares feed,
And hips, and sloes! and on each shallow lake
Making glib slides, where they like shadows go
Till some fresh pastimes in their minds awake.
Then off they start anew and hasty blow
Their numbed and clumpsing fingers till they glow;
Then races with their shadows wildly run
That stride huge giants o'er the shining snow
In the pale splendour of the winter sun.

Childhood

Oh what a wilderness were this sad world
If man were always man, and never child;
If Nature gave no time, so sweetly wild,
When every thought is deftly crisped and curled,
Like fragrant hyacinth with dew impearled,
And every feeling in itself confiding,
Yet never single, but continuous, gliding
With wavy motion as, on wings unfurled,
A seraph clips Empyreal! Such man was
Ere sin had made him know himself too well.
No child was born ere that primeval loss.
What might have been no living soul can tell:
But Heaven is kind, and therefore all possess
Once in their life fair Eden's simpleness.

To a Deaf and Dumb Little Girl

Like a loose island on the wide expanse,
Unconscious floating on the fickle sea,
Herself her all, she lives in privacy;
Her waking life as lonely as a trance,
Doom'd to behold the universal dance,
And never hear the music which expounds
The solemn step, coy slide, the merry bounds,
The vague, mute language of the countenance.
In vain for her I smooth my antic rhyme;
She cannot hear it. All her little being
Concentred in her solitary seeing—
What can she know of beauty or sublime?
And yet methinks she looks so calm and good,
God must be with her in her solitude!

'Long time a child, and still a child, when years'

Long time a child, and still a child, when years
Had painted manhood on my cheek, was I,—
For yet I lived like one not born to die;
A thriftless prodigal of smiles and tears,
No hope I needed, and I knew no fears.
But sleep, though sweet, is only sleep, and waking,
I waked to sleep no more, at once o'ertaking
The vanguard of my age, with all arrears
Of duty on my back. Nor child, nor man,
Nor youth, nor sage, I find my head is grey,
For I have lost the race I never ran:
A rathe December blights my lagging May;
And still I am a child, tho' I be old,
Time is my debtor for my years untold.

On an Infant

Which died before Baptism

'Be, rather than be called, a child of God,'
Death whispered! With assenting nod,
Its head upon its mother's breast,
   The Baby bowed, without demur—
Of the kingdom of the Blest
   Possessor, not Inheritor.

Metrical Feet

Lesson for a Boy

Trōchĕe trīps frŏm lōng tŏ shōrt;
From long to long in solemn sort
Slōw Spōndēe stālks; strōng foot! yet ill able
Ēvĕr to cōme ŭp wĭth Dāctўl trĭsÿllăblĕ.
Ĭāmbĭcs mārch frŏm shōrt tŏ lōng;—
Wĭth ă leap ănd ă bound thĕ swĭft Anăpæsts thrōng;
One syllable long, with one short at each side,
Ămphĭbrăchўs hāstes wĭth ă stātelў stride;—
Fīrst ănd lāst bēĭng lōng, mĭddlĕ shōrt, Aṁphĭmācer
Strīkes hĭs thūndĕrĭng hoofs līke ă proud hīgh-brĕd Rācer.
If Derwent be innocent, steady and wise,
And delight in the things of earth, water, and skies;
Tender warmth at his heart, with these metres to show it,
With sound sense in his brains, may make Derwent a poet,—
May crown him with fame, and must win him the love
Of his father on earth and his Father above.
　　　My dear, dear child!
Could you stand upon Skiddaw, you would not from its
　　　whole ridge
See a man who so loves you as your fond S. T. Coleridge.

Childhood

I used to think that grown-up people chose
To have stiff backs and wrinkles round their nose,
And veins like small fat snakes on either hand,
On purpose to be grand.
'Till through the banisters I watched one day
My great aunt Etty's friend, who was going away,
And how her onyx beads had come unstrung.
I saw her grope to find them as they rolled;
And then I knew that she was helplessly old,
As I was helplessly young.

from The Borough

Peter Grimes

The Father of Peter a Fisherman – Peter's early Conduct—

Old Peter Grimes made fishing his employ;
His wife he cabin'd with him and his boy,
And seem'd that life laborious to enjoy.
To town came quiet Peter with his fish,
And had of all a civil word and wish.
He left his trade upon the sabbath-day,
And took young Peter in his hand to pray:
But soon the stubborn boy from care broke loose,
At first refused, then added his abuse:
His father's love he scorn'd, his power defied,
But being drunk, wept sorely when he died.

  Yes! then he wept, and to his mind there came
Much of his conduct, and he felt the shame,—
How he had oft the good old man reviled,
And never paid the duty of a child;
How, when the father in his Bible read,
He in contempt and anger left the shed;
'It is the word of life,' the parent cried;
— 'This is the life itself,' the boy replied;
And while old Peter in amazement stood,
Gave the hot spirit to his boiling blood:—
How he, with oath and furious speech, began
To prove his freedom and assert the man;
And when the parent check'd his impious rage,
How he had cursed the tyranny of age;—
Nay, once had dealt the sacrilegious blow
On his bare head, and laid his parent low;
The father groan'd – 'If thou art old,' said he,
'And hast a son – thou wilt remember me:
Thy mother left me in a happy time,
Thou kill'dst not her – Heav'n spares the double crime.'

He takes an Apprentice – The Boy's Suffering and Fate—

Peter had heard there were in London then,—
Still have they being! – workhouse-clearing men,
Who, undisturb'd by feelings just or kind,
Would parish-boys to needy tradesmen bind:
They in their want a trifling sum would take,
And toiling slaves of piteous orphans make.
Such Peter sought, and when a lad was found,
The sum was dealt him, and the slave was bound.
Some few in town observed in Peter's trap
A boy, with jacket blue and woollen cap;
But none inquired how Peter used the rope,
Or what the bruise, that made the stripling stoop;
None could the ridges on his back behold,
None sought him shiv'ring in the winter's cold;
None put the question, – 'Peter, dost thou give
The boy his food? – What, man! the lad must live:
Consider, Peter, let the child have bread,
He'll serve thee better if he's stroked and fed.'
None reason'd thus – and some, on hearing cries,
Said calmly, 'Grimes is at his exercise.'
Pinn'd, beaten, cold, pinch'd, threaten'd, and abused—
His efforts punish'd and his food refused,—
Awake tormented, – soon aroused from sleep,—
Struck if he wept, and yet compell'd to weep,
The trembling boy dropp'd down and strove to pray,
Received a blow, and trembling turn'd away,
Or sobb'd and hid his piteous face; – while he,
The savage master, grinn'd in horrid glee:
He'd now the power he ever loved to show,
A feeling being subject to his blow.
Thus lived the lad, in hunger, peril, pain,
His tears despised, his supplications vain:
Compell'd by fear to lie, by need to steal,
His bed uneasy and unbless'd his meal,
For three sad years the boy his tortures bore,
And then his pains and trials were no more.
'How died he, Peter?' when the people said,
He growl'd – 'I found him lifeless in his bed';
Then tried for softer tone, and sigh'd, 'Poor Sam is dead.'

A Convent School in a Corrupt City

Hark how they laugh, those children at their sport!
O'er all this city vast that knows not sleep
Labour and sin their ceaseless vigil keep:
Yet hither still good angels make resort.
Innocence here and Mirth a single fort
Maintain: and though in many a snake-like sweep
Corruption round the weedy walls doth creep,
Its track not yet hath slimed this sunny court.
Glory to God, who so the world hath framed
That in all places children more abound
Than they by whom Humanity is shamed!
Children outnumber men: and millions die—
Who knows not this? – in blameless infancy
Sowing with innocence our sin-stained ground.

How the waters closed above him

How the waters closed above him
We shall never know;
How he stretched his anguish to us,
That is covered too.

Spreads the pond her base of lilies
Bold above the boy
Whose unclaimèd hat and jacket
Sum the history.

In Mrs Tilscher's Class

You could travel up the Blue Nile
with your finger, tracing the route
while Mrs Tilscher chanted the scenery.
Tana. Ethiopia. Khartoum. Aswân.
That for a hour, then a skittle of milk
and the chalky Pyramids rubbed into dust.
A window opened with a long pole.
The laugh of a bell swung by a running child.

This was better than home. Enthralling books.
The classroom glowed like a sweetshop.
Sugar paper. Coloured shapes. Brady and Hindley
faded, like the faint, uneasy smudge of a mistake.
Mrs Tilscher loved you. Some mornings, you found
she'd left a good gold star by your name.
The scent of a pencil slowly, carefully, shaved.
A xylophone's nonsense heard from another form.

Over the Easter term, the inky tadpoles changed
from commas into exclamation marks. Three frogs
hopped in the playground, freed by a dunce,
followed by a line of kids, jumping and croaking
away from the lunch queue. A rough boy
told you how you were born. You kicked him, but stared
at your parents, appalled, when you got back home.

That feverish July, the air tasted of electricity.
A tangible alarm made you always untidy, hot,
fractious under the heavy, sexy sky. You asked her
how you were born and Mrs Tilscher smiled,
then turned away. Reports were handed out.
You ran through the gates, impatient to be grown,
as the sky split open into a thunderstorm.

'In going to my naked bed, as one that would have slept,'

In going to my naked bed, as one that would have slept,
I heard a wife sing to her child, that long before had wept.
She sighed sore, and sang full sweet, to bring the babe to rest,
That would not cease, but cried still in sucking at her breast.
She was full weary of her watch and grieved with her child,
She rocked it, and rated it, till that on her it smiled.
Then did she say, 'Now have I found this proverb true to prove:
The falling out of faithful friends, renewing is of love.'

Brother and Sister (1)

I cannot choose but think upon the time
    When our two lives grew like two buds that kiss
At lightest thrill from the bee's swinging chime,
    Because the one so near the other is.
He was the elder and a little man
    Of forty inches, bound to show no dread,
And I the girl that puppy-like now ran,
    Now lagged behind my brother's larger tread.
I held him wise, and when he talked to me
    Of snakes and birds, and which God loved the best,
I thought his knowledge marked the boundary
    Where men grew blind, though angels knew the rest.
If he said 'Hush!' I tried to hold my breath;
Wherever he said 'Come!' I stepped in faith.

Brother and Sister (2)

Long years have left their writing on my brow,
    But yet the freshness and the dew-fed beam
Of those young mornings are about me now,
    When we two wandered toward the far-off stream
With rod and line. Our basket held a store
    Baked for us only, and I thought with joy
That I should have my share, though he had more,
    Because he was the elder and a boy.
The firmaments of daisies since to me
    Have had those mornings in their opening eyes,
The bunchèd cowslip's pale transparency
    Carries that sunshine of sweet memories,
And wild-rose branches take their finest scent
From those blest hours of infantine content.

Ruthless Rhymes

The Stern Parent

Father heard his Children scream,
So he threw them in the stream,
Saying, as he drowned the third,
'Children should be seen, *not* heard!'

Tender-Heartedness

Billy, in one of his nice new sashes,
Fell in the fire and was burnt to ashes;
Now, although the room grows chilly,
I haven't the heart to poke poor Billy.

Sephestia's Song to Her Child

(From 'Menaphon.')

Weep not, my wanton, smile upon my knee;
When thou art old, there's grief enough for thee.
        Mother's wag, pretty boy,
        Father's sorrow, father's joy;
        When thy father first did see
        Such a boy by him and me,
        He was glad, I was woe;
        Fortune changèd made him so,
        When he left his pretty boy,
        Last his sorrow, first his joy.

Weep not, my wanton, smile upon my knee;
When thou art old, there's grief enough for thee.
        Streaming tears that never stint,
        Like pearl-drops from a flint,
        Fell by course from his eyes'
        That one another's place supplies;
        Thus he grieved in every part,
        Tears of blood fell from his heart
        When he left his pretty boy,
        Father's sorrow, father's joy.

Weep not, my wanton, smile upon my knee;
When thou art old, there's grief enough for thee.
        The wanton smiled, father wept,
        Mother cried, baby leapt;
        More he crowed, more we cried,
        Nature could not sorrow hide:
        He must go, he must kiss
        Child and mother, baby bliss,
        For he left his pretty boy,
        Father's sorrow, father's joy.
Weep not, my wanton, smile upon my knee;
When thou art old, there's grief enough for thee.

Mid-Term Break

I sat all morning in the college sick bay
Counting bells knelling classes to a close.
At two o'clock our neighbours drove me home.

In the porch I met my father crying—
He had always taken funerals in his stride—
And Big Jim Evans saying it was a hard blow.

The baby cooed and laughed and rocked the pram
When I came in, and I was embarrassed
By old men standing up to shake my hand

And tell me they were 'sorry for my trouble'.
Whispers informed strangers I was the eldest,
Away at school, as my mother held my hand

In hers and coughed out angry tearless sighs.
At ten o'clock the ambulance arrived
With the corpse, stanched and bandaged by the nurses.

Next morning I went up into the room. Snowdrops
And candles soothed the bedside; I saw him
For the first time in six weeks. Paler now,

Wearing a poppy bruise on his left temple,
He lay in the four foot box as in his cot.
No gaudy scars, the bumper knocked him clear,

A four foot box, a foot for every year.

*Casabianca**

The boy stood on the burning deck
  Whence all but he had fled;
The flame that lit the battle's wreck
  Shone round him o'er his head.

Yet beautiful and bright he stood,
  As born to rule the storm—
A creature of heroic blood,
  A proud, though child-like form.

The flames rolled on – he would not go
  Without his father's word;
That father, faint in death below,
  His voice no longer heard.

He called aloud : – 'Say, father, say,
  If yet my task is done!'
He knew not that the chieftain lay
  Unconscious of his son.

'Speak, father!' once again he cried,
  'If I may yet be gone!'
And but the booming shots replied,
  And fast the flames rolled on.

Upon his brow he felt their breath,
  And in his waving hair,
And looked from that lone post of death
  In still yet brave despair.

* Young Casabianca, a boy about thirteen years old, son of the Admiral of
the Orient, remained at his post (in the battle of the Nile) after the ship
had taken fire, and all the guns had been abandoned; and perished in the
explosion of the vessel, when the flames had reached the powder.

And shouted but once more aloud,
  'My father! must I stay?'
While o'er him fast, through sail and shroud,
  The wreathing fires made way.

They wrapt the ship in splendour wild,
  They caught the flag on high,
And streamed above the gallant child
  Like banners in the sky.

There came a burst of thunder-sound—
  The boy – oh! where was he?
Ask of the winds that far around
  With fragments strewed the sea!—

With mast and helm, and pennon fair,
  That well had borne their part;
But the noblest thing which perished there
  Was that young faithful heart!

A Child's Grace

Here a little child I stand
Heaving up my either hand;
Cold as paddocks though they be,
Here I lift them up to Thee,
For a benison to fall
On our meat and on us all. Amen.

Epitaph

upon a Child that died

Here she lies, a pretty bud,
Lately made of flesh and blood:
Who as soon fell fast asleep
As her little eyes did peep.
Give her strewings, but not stir
The earth that lightly covers her.

Another

Here a pretty baby lies
Sung asleep with lullabies:
Pray be silent and not stir
Th' easy earth that covers her.

A Boy's Song

Where the pools are bright and deep,
Where the grey trout lies asleep,
Up the river and over the lea,
That's the way for Billy and me.

Where the blackbird sings the latest,
Where the hawthorn blooms the sweetest,
Where the nestlings chirp and flee,
That's the way for Billy and me.

Where the mowers mow the cleanest,
Where the hay lies thick and greenest,
There to track the homeward bee,
That's the way for Billy and me.

Where the hazel bank is steepest,
Where the shadow falls the deepest,
Where the clustering nuts fall free,
That's the way for Billy and me.

Why the boys should drive away
Little sweet maidens from the play,
Or love to banter and fight so well,
That's the thing I never could tell.

But this I know, I love to play
Through the meadow, among the hay;
Up the water and over the lea,
That's the way for Billy and me.

I Remember, I Remember

I remember, I remember
The house where I was born,
The little window where the sun
Came peeping in at morn;
He never came a wink too soon,
Nor brought too long a day,
But now, I often wish the night
Had borne my breath away!

I remember, I remember
The roses, red and white,
The violets, and the lily-cups,
Those flowers made of light!
The lilac where the robin built,
And where my brother set
The laburnum on his birthday—
The tree is living yet!

I remember, I remember
Where I used to swing,
And thought the air must rush as fresh
To swallows on the wing;
My spirit flew in feathers then,
That is so heavy now,
And summer pools could hardly cool
The fever on my brow!

I remember, I remember
The fir trees dark and high;
I used to think their slender tops
Were close against the sky:
It was a childish ignorance,
But now 'tis little joy
To know I'm farther off from Heav'n
Than when I was a boy.

A Parental Ode to My Son, Aged Three Years and Five Months

Thou happy, happy elf!
(But stop, – first let me kiss away that tear)—
Thou tiny image of myself!
(My love, he's poking peas into his ear!)
Thou merry, laughing sprite!
With spirits feather-light,
Untouched by sorrow and unsoiled by sin—
(Good heavens! the child is swallowing a pin!)

Thou little tricksy Puck!
With antic toys so funnily bestuck,
Light as the singing bird that wings the air—
(The door! the door! he'll tumble down the stair!)
Thou darling of thy sire!
(Why Jane, he'll set his pinafore a-fire!)
Thou imp of mirth and joy!
In love's dear chain so strong and bright a link,
Thou idol of thy parents – (Drat the boy!
There goes my ink!)

Thou cherub but of earth;
Fit playfellow for Fays, by moonlight pale,
In harmless sport and mirth,
(That dog will bite him if he pulls its tail!)
Thou human humming-bee, extracting honey
From every blossom in the world that blows,
Singing in Youth's Elysium ever sunny—
(Another tumble! – that's his precious nose!)

Thy father's pride and hope!
(He'll break the mirror with that skipping-rope!)
With pure heart newly stamped from Nature's mint—
(Where *did* he learn that squint?)

Thou young domestic dove!
(He'll have that jug off, with another shove!)
Dear nursling of the hymeneal nest!
(Are those torn clothes his best?)
Little epitome of man!
(He'll climb upon the table, that's his plan!)
Touched with the beauteous tints of dawning life—
(He's got a knife!)

Thou enviable being!
No storms, no clouds, in thy blue sky foreseeing,
Play on, play on,
My elfin John!
Toss the light ball – bestride the stick—
(I knew so many cakes would make him sick!)
With fancies buoyant as the thistledown,
Prompting the face grotesque, and antic brisk,
With many a lamb-like frisk,
(He's got the scissors, snipping at your gown!)

Thou pretty opening rose!
(Go to your mother, child, and wipe your nose!)
Balmy, and breathing music like the South,
(He really brings my heart into my mouth!)
Fresh as the morn, and brilliant as its star,—
(I wish that window had an iron bar!)
Bold as the hawk, yet gentle as the dove—
(I'll tell you what, my love,
I cannot write, unless he's sent above!)

Man and Boy

Oh, when I was a tiny boy,
My nights and days were full of joy,
    My mates were blithe and kind!—
No wonder that I sometimes sigh,
And dash the tear-drop from my eye,
    To cast a look behind!

A hoop was an eternal round
Of pleasure. In those days I found
    A top a joyous thing;—
But now those past delights I drop,
My head, alas! is all my top,
    And careful thoughts the string!

My joys are wingless all and dead;
My dumps are made of more than lead;
    My flights soon find a fall;
My fears prevail, my fancies droop,
Joy never cometh with a hoop,
    And seldom with a call!

My football's laid upon the shelf;
I am a shuttlecock myself
    The world knocks to and fro;—
My archery is all unlearn'd,
And grief against myself has turn'd
    My arrows and my bow!

No skies so blue or so serene
As then; – no leaves look half so green
    As clothed the playground tree!
All things I loved are alter'd so,
Nor does it ease my heart to know
    That change resides in me!

Spring and Fall

to a young child

Margaret, are you grieving
Over Goldengrove unleaving?
Leaves, like the things of man, you
With your fresh thoughts care for, can you?
Ah! as the heart grows older
It will come to such sights colder
By and by, nor spare a sigh
Though worlds of wanwood leafmeal lie;
And yet you *will* weep and know why.
Now no matter, child, the name:
Sorrow's springs are the same.
Nor mouth had, no nor mind, expressed
What heart heard of, ghost guessed:
It is the blight man was born for,
It is Margaret you mourn for.

Infant Innocence

The Grizzly Bear is huge and wild;
He has devoured the infant child.
The infant child is not aware
He has been eaten by the bear.

The Age of Children Happiest

Laid in my quiet bed in study as I were,
I saw within my troubled head a heap of thoughts appear,
And every thought did show so lively in mine eyes,
That now I sighed, and then I smiled, as cause of thoughts did
    rise.
I saw the little boy in thought, how oft that he
Did wish of God, to 'scape the rod, a tall young man to be;
The young man eke that feels his bones with pain opprest,
How he would be a rich old man, to live and be at rest !
The rich old man that sees his end draw on so sore,
How would he be a boy again to live so much the more.
Whereat full oft I smiled, to see how all those three,
From boy to man, from man to boy, would chop and change
    degree.

Full Moon and Little Frieda

A cool small evening shrunk to a dog bark and the clank
of a bucket—

And you listening.
A spider's web, tense for the dew's touch.
A pail lifted, still and brimming – mirror
To tempt a first star to a tremor.

Cows are going home in the lane there, looping the hedges
with their warm wreaths of breath—
A dark river of blood, many boulders,
Balancing unspilled milk.

'Moon!' you cry suddenly, 'Moon! Moon!'

The moon has stepped back like an artist gazing amazed
at a work

That points at him amazed.

To T. L. H.

Six years old, during a sickness

Sleep breathes at last from out thee,
　My little, patient boy;
And balmy rest about thee
　Smooths off the day's annoy.
　　I sit me down, and think
　Of all thy winning ways;
Yet almost wish, with sudden shrink,
　That I had less to praise.

Thy sidelong pillowed meekness,
　Thy thanks to all that aid,
Thy heart, in pain and weakness,
　Of fancied faults afraid;
　　The little trembling hand
　That wipes thy quiet tears,—
These, these are things that may demand
　Dread memories for years.

Sorrows I've had, severe ones,
　I will not think of now:
And calmly, midst my dear ones,
　Have wasted with dry brow;
　　But when thy fingers press
　And pat my stooping head,
I cannot bear the gentleness,—
　The tears are in their bed.

Ah, first-born of thy mother,
   When life and hope were new,
Kind playmate of thy brother,
   Thy sister, father too;
     My light, where'er I go,
   My bird, when prison-bound,
My hand in hand companion, – no,
   My prayers shall hold thee round.

To say 'He has departed'—
   'His voice' – 'his face' – is gone;
To feel impatient-hearted,
   Yet feel we must bear on;
     Ah, I could not endure
   To whisper of such woe,
Unless I felt this sleep ensure
   That it will not be so.

Yes, still he's fixed and sleeping!
   This silence too the while—
Its very hush and creeping
   Seem whispering us a smile:
     Something divine and dim
   Seems going by one's ear,
Like parting wings of Cherubim,
   Who say, 'We've finished here.'

On My First Daughter

Here lies, to each her parents' ruth,
Mary, the daughter of their youth;
Yet all heaven's gifts being heaven's due,
It makes the father less to rue.
At six months' end she parted hence,
With safety of her innocence;
Whose soul Heaven's queen (whose name she bears),
In comfort of her mother's tears,
Hath placed among her virgin train:
Where, while that, severed, doth remain,
This grave partakes the fleshly birth;
Which cover lightly, gentle earth!

On My First Son

Farewell, thou child of my right hand, and joy:
    My sin was too much hope of thee, loved boy:
Seven years thou wert lent to me, and I thee pay,
    Exacted by thy faith on the just day.
O, could I lose all father now ! for why
    Will man lament the state he should envy?
To have so soon 'scaped world's and flesh's rage,
    And if no other misery, yet age!
Rest in soft peace, and asked, say here doth lie
    Ben Jonson his best piece of poetry,
For whose sake henceforth all his vows be such
    As what he loves may never like too much.

The Old Familiar Faces

I have had playmates, I have had companions,
In my days of childhood, in my joyful school-days,
All, all are gone, the old familiar faces.

I have been laughing, I have been carousing,
Drinking late, sitting late, with my bosom cronies,
All, all are gone, the old familiar faces.

I loved a love once, fairest among women:
Closed are her doors on me, I must not see her—
All, all are gone, the old familiar faces.

I have a friend, a kinder friend has no man;
Like an ingrate, I felt my friend abruptly;
Left him, to muse on the old familiar faces.

Ghost-like I paced round the haunts of my childhood,
Earth seemed a desert I was bound to traverse,
Seeking to find the old familiar faces.

Friend of my bosom, thou more than a brother,
Why wert not thou born in my father's dwelling?
So might we talk of the old familiar faces—

How some they have died, and some they have left me,
And some are taken from me; all are departed;
All, all are gone, the old familiar faces.

Childhood

In my poor mind it is most sweet to muse
Upon the days gone by; to act in thought
Past seasons o'er, and be again a child;
To sit in fancy on the turf-clad slope
Down which the child would roll; to pluck gay flowers,
Make posies in the sun, which the child's hand
(Childhood offended soon, soon reconciled)
Would throw away, and straight take up again,
Then fling them to the winds, and o'er the lawn
Bound with so playful and so light a foot,
That the pressed daisy scarce declined her head.

Feigned Courage

Horatio, of ideal courage vain,
Was flourishing in air his father's cane,
And, as the fumes of valour swelled his pate,
Now thought himself *this* hero, and now *that;*
　'And now,' he cried, 'I will Achilles be;
My sword I brandish, see, the Trojans flee.
Now I'll be Hector when his angry blade
A lane through heaps of slaughtered Grecians made!
And now by deeds still braver I'll convince,
I am no less than Edward the Black Prince.
Give way, ye coward French!' As thus he spoke,
And aimed in fancy a sufficient stroke
To fix the fate of Cressy or Poictiers
(The nurse relates the hero's fate with tears);
He struck his milk-white hand against a nail,
Sees his own blood, and feels his courage fail.
Ah! where is now that boasted valour flown,
That in the tented field so late was shown?
Achilles weeps, great Hector hangs his head!
And the Black Prince goes whimpering to bed.

Before a Saint's Picture

My serious son! I see thee look
First on the picture, then the book.
I catch the wish that thou couldst paint
The yearnings of the ecstatic saint.
Give it not up, my serious son!
Wish it again, and it is done.
Seldom will any fail who tries
With patient hand and steadfast eyes,
And woos the true with such pure sighs.

Different Graces

Around the child bend all the three
Sweet Graces – Faith, Hope, Charity.
Around the man bend other faces—
Pride, Envy, Malice, are his Graces.

A Terrible Infant

I recollect a nurse called Ann,
  Who carried me about the grass,
And one fine day a fair young man
  Came up and kissed the pretty lass:
She did not make the least objection!
      Thinks I, *Aha!*
When I can talk I'll tell Mamma!
—And that's my earliest recollection.

The Children's Hour

Between the dark and the daylight,
    When the night is beginning to lower,
Comes a pause in the day's occupation,
    That is known as the Children's Hour.

I hear in the chamber above me
    The patter of little feet,
The sound of a door that is opened,
    And voices soft and sweet.

From my study I see in the lamplight,
    Descending the broad hall stair,
Grave Alice and laughing Allegra,
    And Edith with golden hair.

A whisper and then a silence;
    Yet I know by their merry eyes
They are plotting and planning together
    To take me by surprise.

A sudden rush from the stairway,
    A sudden raid from the hall!
By three doors left unguarded
    They enter my castle wall!

They climb up into my turret
    O'er the arms and back of my chair;
If I try to escape they surround me;
    They seem to be everywhere.

They almost devour me with kisses,
    Their arms about me entwine,
Till I think of the Bishop of Bingen
    In his Mouse Tower on the Rhine!

Do you think, O blue-eyed banditti,
    Because you have scaled the wall,
Such an old moustache as I am
    Is not a match for you all!

I have you fast in my fortress,
  And will not let you depart,
But put you down into the dungeon
  In the round-tower of my heart.

And there will I keep you for ever,
  Yes, for ever and a day,
Till the walls shall crumble to ruin,
  And moulder in dust away!

from The Song of Hiawatha

III. Hiawatha's Childhood

By the shores of Gitche Gumee,
By the shining Big-Sea-Water,
Stood the wigwam of Nokomis,
Daughter of the Moon, Nokomis.
Dark behind it rose the forest,
Rose the black and gloomy pine-trees,
Rose the firs with cones upon them;
Bright before it beat the water,
Beat the clear and sunny water,
Beat the shining Big-Sea-Water.

There the wrinkled, old Nokomis
Nursed the little Hiawatha,
Rocked him in his linden cradle,
Bedded soft in moss and rushes,
Safely bound with reindeer sinews ...

Many things Nokomis taught him
Of the stars that shine in heaven;
Showed him Ishkoodah, the comet,
Ishkoodah, with fiery tresses;
Showed the Death-Dance of the spirits,
Warriors with their plumes and war-clubs,
Flaring far away to northward
In the frosty nights of Winter;
Showed the broad, white road in heaven,
Pathway of the ghosts, the shadows,
Running straight across the heavens,
Crowded with the ghosts, the shadows.

At the door on summer evenings
Sat the little Hiawatha;
Heard the whispering of the pine-trees,
Heard the lapping of the water,

Sounds of music, words of wonder:
'Minne-wawa!' said the pine-trees,
'Mudway-aushka!' said the water . . .

   Saw the moon rise from the water
Rippling, rounding from the water,
Saw the flecks and shadows on it,
Whispered, 'What is that, Nokomis?'
And the good Nokomis answered:
'Once a warrior, very angry,
Seized his grandmother, and threw her
Up into the sky at midnight;
Right against the moon he threw her;
'Tis her body that you see there . . .'

   When he heard the owls at midnight,
Hooting, laughing in the forest,
'What is that?' he cried in terror;
'What is that?' he said, 'Nokomis?'
And the good Nokomis answered:
'That is but the owl and owlet,
Talking in their native language,
Talking, scolding at each other.'

   Then the little Hiawatha
Learned of every bird its language,
Learned their names and all their secrets,
How they built their nests in Summer,
Where they hid themselves in Winter,
Talked with them whene'er he met them,
Called them 'Hiawatha's Chickens'.
Of all beasts he learned the language,
Learned their names and all their secrets,
How the beavers built their lodges,
Where the squirrels hid their acorns,
How the reindeer ran so swiftly,
Why the rabbit was so timid,
Talked with them whene'er he met them,
Called them 'Hiawatha's Brothers' . . .

The Wreck of the Hesperus

It was the schooner Hesperus,
   That sailed the wintry sea;
And the skipper had taken his little daughter,
   To bear him company.

Blue were her eyes as the fairy-flax,
   Her cheeks like the dawn of day,
And her bosom white as the hawthorn buds,
   That ope in the month of May.

The skipper he stood beside the helm,
   His pipe was in his mouth,
And he watched how the veering flaw did blow
   The smoke now West, now South.

Then up and spake an old Sailòr,
   Had sailed the Spanish Main,
'I pray thee, put into yonder port,
   For I fear a hurricane.

'Last night the moon had a golden ring,
   And to-night no moon we see!'
The skipper he blew a whiff from his pipe,
   And a scornful laugh laughed he.

Colder and louder blew the wind,
   A gale from the North-cast;
The snow fell hissing in the brine,
   And the billows frothed like yeast.

Down came the storm, and smote amain
   The vessel in its strength;
She shuddered and paused, like a frighted steed,
   Then leaped her cable's length.

'Come hither! come hither! my little daughter,
    And do not tremble so;
For I can weather the roughest gale
    That ever wind did blow.'

He wrapped her warm in his seaman's coat,
    Against the stinging blast;
He cut a rope from a broken spar,
    And bound her to the mast.

'O father! I hear the church-bells ring,
    O say what may it be?'
''Tis a fog-bell on a rock-bound coast!'—
    And he steered for the open sea.

'O father! I hear the sound of guns,
    O say, what may it be?'
'Some ship in distress, that cannot live
    In such an angry sea!'

'O father! I see a gleaming light,
    O say, what may it be?'
But the father answered never a word,
    A frozen corpse was he.

Lashed to the helm, all stiff and stark,
    With his face turned to the skies,
The lantern gleamed through the gleaming snow
    On his fixed and glassy eyes.

Then the maiden clasped her hands and prayed,
    That savèd she might be;
And she thought of Christ, who stilled the wave,
    On the Lake of Galilee.

And fast through the midnight dark and drear,
    Through the whistling sleet and snow,
Like a sheeted ghost the vessel swept
    Tow'rds the reef of Norman's Woe.

And ever the fitful gusts between,
    A sound came from the land;
It was the sound of the trampling surf,
    On the rocks and the hard sea-sand.

The breakers were right beneath her bows,
    She drifted a dreary wreck,
And a whooping billow swept the crew
    Like icicles from her deck.

She struck where the white and fleecy waves
    Looked soft as carded wool,
But the cruel rocks, they gored her side
    Like the horns of an angry bull.

Her rattling shrouds, all sheathed in ice,
    With the masts went by the board;
Like a vessel of glass, she stove and sank,
    Ho! ho! the breakers roared!

At daybreak, on the black sea-beach,
    A fisherman stood aghast,
To see the form of a maiden fair,
    Lashed close to a drifting mast

The salt sea was frozen on her breast,
    The salt tears in her eyes;
And he saw her hair, like the brown sea-weed,
    On the billows fall and rise.

Such was the wreck of the Hesperus,
    In the midnight and the snow;
Christ save us all from a death like this,
    On the reef of Norman's Woe!

Maidenhood

Maiden! with the meek, brown eyes,
In whose orbs a shadow lies
Like the dusk in evening skies!

Thou whose locks outshine the sun,
Golden tresses, wreathed in one,
As the braided streamlets run!

Standing, with reluctant feet,
Where the brook and river meet,
Womanhood and childhood fleet!

Gazing, with a timid glance,
On the brooklet's swift advance,
On the river's broad expanse!

Deep and still, that gliding stream
Beautiful to thee must seem,
As the river of a dream.

Then why pause with indecision,
When bright angels in thy vision
Beckon thee to fields Elysian?

Seest thou shadows sailing by,
As the dove, with startled eye,
Sees the falcon's shadow fly?

Hearest thou voices on the shore,
That our ears perceive no more,
Deafened by the cataract's roar?

Oh, thou child of many prayers!
Life hath quicksands, – Life hath snares!
Care and age come unawares!

Like the swell of some sweet tune,
Morning rises into noon,
May glides onward into June.

Childhood is the bough, where slumbered
Birds and blossoms many-numbered;—
Age, that bough with snows encumbered.

Gather, then, each flower that grows,
When the young heart overflows,
To embalm that tent of snows.

Bear a lily in thy hand;
Gates of brass cannot withstand
One touch of that magic wand.

Bear through sorrow, wrong, and ruth,
In thy heart the dew of youth,
On thy lips the smile of truth.

Oh, that dew, like balm, shall steal
Into wounds that cannot heal,
Even as sleep our eyes doth seal;

And that smile, like sunshine, dart
Into many a sunless heart,
For a smile of God thou art.

Autobiography

In my childhood trees were green
And there was plenty to be seen.
Come back early or never come.

My father made the walls resound,
He wore his collar the wrong way round.
Come back early or never come.

My mother wore a yellow dress,
Gently, gently, gentleness.
Come back early or never come.

When I was five the black dreams came;
Nothing after that was quite the same.
Come back early or never come.

The dark was talking to the dead;
The lamp was dark beside my bed.
Come back early or never come.

When I woke they did not care,
Nobody, nobody was there.
Come back early or never come.

When my silent terror cried
Nobody, nobody replied.
Come back early or never come.

I got up; the chilly sun
Saw me walk away alone.
Come back early or never come.

The Picture of little T. C. in a Prospect of Flowers

See with what simplicity
This Nimph begins her golden daies!
In the green Grass she loves to lie,
And there with her fair Aspect tames
The Wilder Flow'rs, and gives them names:
But only with the Roses playes;
       And them does tell
What Colour best becomes them, and what Smell.

Who can foretell for what high cause
This Darling of the Gods was born!
Yet this is She whose chaster Laws
The wanton Love shall one day fear,
And, under her command severe,
See his Bow broke and Ensigns torn.
       Happy, who can
Appease this virtuous Enemy of Man!

O then let me in time compound,
And parly with those conquering Eyes;
Ere they have try'd their force to wound,
Ere, with their glancing wheels, they drive
In Triumph over Hearts that strive,
And them that yield but more despise.
       Let me be laid,
Where I may see thy Glories from some Shade.

Mean time, whilst every verdant thing
It self does at thy Beauty charm,
Reform the errours of the Spring;
Make that the Tulips may have share
Of sweetness, seeing they are fair;

And Roses of their thorns disarm:
                    But most procure
That Violets may a longer Age endure.

But O young beauty of the Woods,
Whom Nature courts with fruits and flow'rs,
Gather the Flow'rs, but spare the Buds;
Lest *Flora* angry at the crime,
To kill her Infants in their prime,
Do quickly make th' Example Yours;
                    And, ere we see,
Nip in the blossome all our hopes and Thee.

Young Love

Come little Infant, Love me now,
    While thine unsuspected years
Clear thine aged Father's brow
    From cold Jealousie and Fears.

Pretty surely 'twere to see
    By young Love old Time beguil'd:
While our Sportings are as free
    As the Nurses with the Child.

Common beauties stay fifteen;
    Such as yours should swifter move;
Whose fair Blossoms are too green
    Yet for Lust, but not for Love.

Love as much the snowy Lamb
    Or the wanton Kid does prize,
As the lusty Bull or Ram,
    For his morning Sacrifice.

Now then love me: time may take
    Thee before thy time away:
Of this Need we'll Virtue make,
    And learn Love before we may.

So we win of doubtful Fate;
    And, if good she to us meant,
We that Good shall antedate,
    Or, if ill, that Ill prevent.

Thus as Kingdomes, frustrating
    Other Titles to their Crown,
In the craddle crown their King,
    So all Forraign Claims to drown,

So, to make all Rivals vain,
    Now I crown thee with my Love:
Crown me with thy Love again,
    And we both shall Monarchs prove.

To a Boy

with a watch

Written for a Friend

Is it not sweet, beloved youth,
   To rove through Erudition's bowers,
And cull the golden fruits of truth,
   And gather Fancy's brilliant flowers?

And is it not more sweet than this,
   To feel thy parents' hearts approving,
And pay them back in sums of bliss
   The dear, the endless debt of loving?

It must be so to thee, my youth;
   With this idea toil is lighter;
This sweetens all the fruits of truth,
   And makes the flowers of fancy brighter

The little gift we send thee, boy,
   May sometimes teach thy soul to ponder,
If indolence or syren joy
   Should ever tempt that soul to wander.

'Twill tell thee that the winged day
   Can ne'er be chain'd by man's endeavour,
That life and time shall fade away,
   While heav'n and virtue bloom for ever.

It is Indeed Spinach

People by whom I am riled
Are people who go around wishing O that Time would
    backward turn backward and again make them a child.
Either they have no sense, or else they go round repeating
    something they have heard like a parakeet,
Or else they deliberately prevarikete.
Because into being a marathon dancer or a chiropodist or a tea-
    taster or a certified public accountant I would not be
    beguiled,
But I would sooner than I would into being again a child,
Because being a child is not much of a pastime,
And I don't want any next time because I remember the last
    time.
I do not wish to play with my toes,
Nor do I wish to have cod-liver oil spooned down my throat or
    albolene pushed up my nose.
I don't want to be plopped down at sundown into a crib or a
    cradle
And if I don't go to sleep right away to be greeted with either a
    lullaby or an upbraidal.
I can think of nothing worse
Than never being out of sight of a parent or a nurse;
Yes, that is the part that I don't see how they survive it,
To have their private life so far from private.
Furthermore, I don't want to cry for the moon,
And I do want to hold my own spoon;
I have more ambitious ideas of a lark
Than to collect pebbles in my hat or be taken for a walk in the
    park;
I should hate to be held together with safety pins instead of
    buttons and suspenders and belts,

And I should particularly hate being told every time I was doing
    something I liked that it was time to do something else.
So it's pooh for the people who want Time to make them a child
    again, because I think that they must already be a child again
    or else they would stand up and own up
That it's much more fun to be a grown-up.

Vitaï Lampada (The Torch of Life)

There's a breathless hush in the Close tonight—
       Ten to make and the match to win—
A bumping pitch and a blinding light,
       An hour to play and the last man in.
And it's not for the sake of a ribboned coat,
       Or the selfish hope of a season's fame,
But his Captain's hand on his shoulder smote—
       'Play up! Play up! And play the game!'

The sand of the desert is sodden red,—
       Red with the wreck of a square that broke;—
The Gatling's jammed and the Colonel dead,
       And the regiment blind with dust and smoke.
The river of death has brimmed his banks,
       And England's far, and Honour a name,
But the voice of a schoolboy rallies the ranks:
       'Play up! Play up! And play the game!'

This is the word that year by year,
       While in her place the School is set,
Ever   y one of her sons must hear,
    And none that hears it dare forget.
This they all with a joyful mind
       Bear through life like a torch in flame,
And falling fling to the host behind—
       'Play up! Play up! And play the game!'

The Toys

My little Son, who look'd from thoughtful eyes,
And moved and spoke in quiet grown-up wise,
Having my law the seventh time disobey'd,
I struck him, and dismiss'd
With hard words and unkiss'd,
His mother, who was patient, being dead.
Then, fearing lest his grief should hinder sleep,
I visited his bed,
But found him slumbering deep,
With darken'd eyelids, and their lashes yet
From his late sobbing wet.
And I, with moan,
Kissing away his tears, left others of my own;
For, on a table drawn beside his head,
He had put, within his reach,
A box of counters and a red-veined stone,
A piece of glass abraded by the beach,
And six or seven shells,
A bottle with bluebells,
And two French copper coins, ranged there with careful art
To content his sad heart.
So when that night I pray'd
To God, I wept, and said:
Ah, when at last we lie with trancèd breath,
Not vexing Thee in death,
And thou rememberest of what toys
We made our joys,
How weakly understood,
Thy great commanded good,
Then, fatherly not less
Than I whom Thou hast moulded from the clay,
Thou'lt leave Thy wrath, and say,
'I will be sorry for their childishness.'

To Miss *Charlotte Pulteney* in her *Mother's Arms*

Timely blossom, infant fair,
Fondling of a happy pair,
Every morn and every night,
Their solicitous delight,
Sleeping, waking, still at ease,
Pleasing, without skill to please,
Little gossip, blithe and hale,
Tattling many a broken tale,
Singing many a tuneless song,
Lavish of a heedless tongue,
Simple maiden, void of art,
Babbling out the very heart,
Yet abandoned to thy will,
Yet imagining no ill,
Yet too innocent to blush,
Like the linnet in the bush,
To the mother-linnet's note
Moduling her slender throat,
Chirping forth thy petty joys,
Wanton in the change of toys,
Like the linnet green in May,
Flitting to each bloomy spray,
Wearied then, and glad of rest,
Like the linnet in the nest.
This thy present happy lot,
This, in time, will be forgot:
Other pleasures, other cares,
Ever-busy time prepares;
And thou shalt in thy daughter see
This picture, once, resembled thee.

from Childhood's Hour

From childhood's hour I have not been
As others were; I have not seen
As others saw; I could not bring
My passions from a common spring.
From the same source I have not taken
My sorrow; I could not awaken
My heart to joy at the same tone;
And all I loved, I loved alone.
Then – in my childhood, in the dawn
Of a most stormy life – was drawn
From every depth of good and ill
The mystery which binds me still:
From the torrent or the fountain,
From the red cliff of the mountain,
From the sun that round me rolled
In its autumn tint of gold,
From the lightning in the sky
As it passed me flying by,
From the thunder and the storm,
And the cloud that took the form
(When the rest of Heaven was blue)
Of a demon in my view.

Dreams

Oh! that my young life were a lasting dream!
My spirit not awakening, till the beam
Of an Eternity should bring the morrow.
Yes! tho' that long dream were of hopeless sorrow,
'Twere better than the cold reality
Of waking life, to him whose heart must be,
And hath been still, upon the lovely earth,
A chaos of deep passion, from his birth.

But should it be – that dream eternally
Continuing – as dreams have been to me
In my young boyhood – should it thus be given,
'Twere folly still to hope for higher Heaven.
For I have revell'd when the sun was bright
I' the summer sky, in dreams of living light,
And loveliness, – have left my very heart
In climes of mine imagining, apart
From mine own home, with beings that have been
Of mine own thought – what more could I have seen?

'Twas once – and only once – and the wild hour
From my remembrance shall not pass – some power
Or spell had bound me – 'twas the chilly wind
Came o'er me in the night, and left behind
Its image on my spirit – or the moon
Shone on my slumbers in her lofty noon
Too coldly – or the stars – howe'er it was
That dream was as that night-wind – let it pass.

I *have been* happy, tho' but in a dream.
I have been happy – and I love the theme:
Dreams! in their vivid colouring of life
As in that fleeting, shadowy, misty strife
Of semblance with reality which brings
To the delirious eye, more lovely things
Of Paradise and Love – and all our own!
Than young Hope in his sunniest hour hath known.

School and Schoolfellows

Twelve years ago I made a mock
   Of filthy trades and traffics,
I wonder'd what they meant by stock;
   I wrote delightful sapphics:
I knew the streets of Rome and Troy,
   I supp'd with Fates and Furies,—
Twelve years ago I was a boy,
   A happy boy, at Drury's.

Twelve years ago! – how many a thought
   Of faded pains and pleasures
Those whisper'd syllables have brought
   From memory's hoarded treasures!
The fields, the farms, the bats, the books,
   The glories and disgraces,
The voices of dear friends, the looks
   Of old familiar faces!

Kind *Mater* smiles again to me,
   As bright as when we parted;
I seem again the frank, the free,
   Stout-limb'd, and simple hearted!
Pursuing every idle dream,
   And shunning every warning;
With no hard work but Bovney stream,
   No chill except Long Morning:

Now stopping Harry Vernon's ball
   That rattled like a rocket;
Now hearing Wentworth's 'Fourteen all!'
   And striking for the pocket;
Now feasting on a cheese and flitch,—
   Now drinking from the pewter;
Now leaping over Chalvey ditch,
   Now laughing at my tutor.

Where are my friends? I am alone;
　　No playmate shares my beaker;
Some lie beneath the churchyard stone,
　　And some – before the Speaker;
And some compose a tragedy,
　　And some compose a rondo;
And some draw sword for Liberty,
　　And some draw pleas for John Doe.

Tom Mill was used to blacken eyes
　　Without the fear of sessions;
Charles Medlar loathed false quantities,
　　As much as false professions;
Now Mill keeps order in the land,
　　A magistrate pedantic;
And Medlar's feet repose unscann'd
　　Beneath the wide Atlantic.

Wild Nick, whose oaths made such a din,
　　Does Dr Martext's duty;
And Mullion, with that monstrous chin,
　　Is married to a Beauty;
And Darrell studies, week by week,
　　His Mant, and not his Manton;
And Ball, who was but poor at Greek,
　　Is very rich at Canton.

And I am eight-and-twenty now;—
　　The world's cold chains have bound me;
And darker shades are on my brow,
　　And sadder scenes around me;
In Parliament I fill my seat,
　　With many other noodles;
And lay my head in Jermyn Street,
　　And sip my hock at Boodle's.

But often, when the cares of life
   Have set my temples aching,
When visions haunt me of a wife,
   When duns await my waking,
When Lady Jane is in a pet,
   Or Hoby in a hurry,
When Captain Hazard wins a bet,
   Or Beaulieu spoils a curry,—

For hours and hours I think and talk
   Of each remember'd hobby;
I long to lounge in Poet's Walk,
   To shiver in the Lobby;
I wish that I could run away
   From House, and Court, and Leveé,
Where bearded men appear to-day
   Just Eton boys grown heavy,—

That I could bask in childhood's sun
   And dance o'er childhood's roses,
And find huge wealth in one pound one,
   Vast wit in broken noses,
And play Sir Giles at Datchet Lane,
   And call the milkmaids Houris,—
That I could be a boy again,—
   A happy boy, – at Drury's.

Childhood and His Visitors

Once on a time, when sunny May
   Was kissing up the April showers,
I saw fair Childhood hard at play
   Upon a bank of blushing flowers:
Happy – he knew not whence or how, –
   And smiling, – who could choose but love him?
For not more glad than Childhood's brow,
   Was the blue heaven that beam'd above him.

Old Time, in most appalling wrath,
   That valley's green repose invaded;
The brooks grew dry upon his path,
   The birds were mute, the lilies faded.
But Time so swiftly wing'd his flight,
   In haste a Grecian tomb to batter,
That Childhood watch'd his paper kite,
   And knew just nothing of the matter.

With curling lip and glancing eye
   Guilt gazed upon the scene a minute;
But Childhood's glance of purity
   Had such a holy spell within it,
That the dark demon to the air
   Spread forth again his baffled pinion,
And hid his envy and despair,
   Self-tortured, in his own dominion.

Then stepp'd a gloomy phantom up,
   Pale, cypress-crown'd, Night's awful daughter,
And proffer'd him a fearful cup
   Full to the brim of bitter water:
Poor Childhood bade her tell her name;
   And when the beldame mutter'd – 'Sorrow,'
He said, – 'Don't interrupt my game;
   I'll taste it, if I must, to-morrow.'

The Muse of Pindus thither came,
   And woo'd him with the softest numbers
That ever scatter'd wealth and fame
   Upon a youthful poet's slumbers;
Though sweet the music of the lay,
   To Childhood it was all a riddle,
And 'Oh,' he cried, 'do send away
   That noisy woman with the fiddle!'

Then Wisdom stole his bat and ball,
   And taught him, with most sage endeavour,
Why bubbles rise and acorns fall,
   And why no toy may last for ever.
She talk'd of all the wondrous laws
   Which Nature's open book discloses,
And Childhood, ere she made a pause,
   Was fast asleep among the roses.

Sleep on, sleep on! oh! Manhood's dreams
   Are all of earthly pain or pleasure,
Of Glory's toils, Ambition's schemes,
   Of cherish'd love, or hoarded treasure:
But to the couch where Childhood lies
   A more delicious trance is given,
Lit up by rays from seraph eyes,
   And glimpses of remember'd Heaven!

To a Child of Quality

Five Years Old; The Author Forty

Lords, knights, and squires, the num'rous band,
    That wear the fair Miss *Mary's* fetters,
Were summon'd, by her high command,
    To show their passions by their letters.

My pen amongst the rest I took,
    Lest those bright eyes that cannot read
Shou'd dart their kindling fires, and look,
    The power they have to be obey'd.

Nor quality, nor reputation,
    Forbid me yet my flame to tell,
Dear five years old befriends my passion,
    And I may write till she can spell.

For while she makes her silk-worms beds
    With all the tender things I swear,
Whilst all the house my passion reads,
    In papers round her baby's hair,

She may receive and own my flame,
    For tho' the strictest prudes shou'd know it,
She'll pass for a most virtuous dame,
    And I for an unhappy poet.

Then too alas! when she shall tear
    The lines some younger rival sends,
She'll give me leave to write I fear,
    And we shall still continue friends;

For, as our diff'rent ages move,
    'Tis so ordain'd, wou'd fate but mend it,
That I shall be past making love
    When she begins to comprehend it.

To My Son

Three things there be that prosper all apace
And flourish, while they grow asunder far;
But on a day, they meet all in a place,
And when they meet they one another mar.
And they be these: the Wood, the Weed, the Wag.
The Wood is that that makes the gallows tree;
The Weed is that that strings the hangman's bag;
The Wag, my pretty knave, betokens thee.
Now mark, dear boy – while these assemble not,
Green springs the tree, hemp grows, the wag is wild;
But when they meet, it makes the timber rot,
It frets the halter, and it chokes the child.
Then bless thee, and beware, and let us pray
We part not with thee at this meeting-day.

Buds and Babies

A million buds are born that never blow,
  That sweet with promise lift a pretty head,
To blush and wither on a barren bed,
  And leave no fruit to show.

Sweet, unfulfilled. Yet have I understood
  One joy, by their fragility made plain:
Nothing was ever beautiful in vain,
  Or all in vain was good.

Lullaby of an Infant Chief

O hush thee, my babie, thy sire was a knight,
Thy mother a lady, both lovely and bright;
The woods and the glens, from the towers which we see,
They all are belonging, dear babie, to thee.
       O ho ro, i ri ri, cadul gu lo,
       O ho ro, i ri ri, &c

O fear not the bugle, though loudly it blows,
It calls but the warders that guard thy repose;
Their bows would be bended, their blades would be red,
Ere the step of a foeman drew near to thy bed.
       O ho ro, i ri ri, &c.

O hush thee, my babie, the time soon will come
When thy sleep shall be broken by trumpet and drum;
Then hush thee, my darling, take rest while you may,
For strife comes with manhood, and waking with day.
       O ho ro, i ri ri, &c.

To William Shelley

I

The billows on the beach are leaping around it,
    The bark is weak and frail,
The sea looks black, and the clouds that bound it
    Darkly strew the gale.
Come with me, thou delightful child,
Come with me, though the wave is wild,
And the winds are loose, we must not stay,
Or the slaves of the law may rend thee away.

II

They have taken thy brother and sister dear,
    They have made them unfit for thee;
They have withered the smile and dried the tear
    Which should have been sacred to me.
To a blighting faith and a cause of crime
They have bound them slaves in youthly prime,
And they will curse my name and thee
Because we fearless are and free.

III

Come thou, belovèd as thou art;
    Another sleepeth still
Near thy sweet mother's anxious heart,
    Which thou with joy shalt fill,
With fairest smiles of wonder thrown
On that which is indeed our own,
And which in distant lands will be
The dearest playmate unto thee.

IV

Fear not the tyrants will rule for ever,
    Or the priests of the evil faith;
They stand on the brink of that raging river,
    Whose waves they have tainted with death.
It is fed from the depths of a thousand dells,
Around them it foams and rages and swells;
And their swords and their sceptres I floating see,
Like wrecks on the surge of eternity.

V

Rest, rest, and shriek not, thou gentle child!
    The rocking of the boat thou fearest,
And the cold spray and the clamour wild?—
    There, sit between us two, thou dearest—
Me and thy mother – well we know
The storm at which thou tremblest so,
With all its dark and hungry graves,
Less cruel than the savage slaves
Who hunt us o'er these sheltering waves.

VI

This hour will in thy memory
    Be a dream of days forgotten long.
We soon shall dwell by the azure sea
Of serene and golden Italy,
Or Greece, the Mother of the free;
    And I will teach thine infant tongue
To call upon those heroes old
In their own language, and will mould
Thy growing spirit in the flame
Of Grecian lore, that by such name
A patriot's birthright thou mayst claim!

The Truant

Wee Sandy in the corner
   Sits greeting on a stool,
And sair the laddie rues
   Playing truant frae the school;
Then ye'll learn frae silly Sandy,
   Wha's gotten sic a fright,
To do naething through the day
   That may gar ye greet at night.

He durstna venture hame now,
   Nor play, though e'er so fine,
And ilka ane he met wi'
   He thought them sure to ken,
And started at ilk whin bush,
   Though it was braid daylight—
Sae do naething through the day
   That may gar ye greet at night.

Wha winna be advised
   Are sure to rue ere lang;
And muckle pains it costs them
   To do the thing that's wrang,
When they wi' half the fash o't
   Might aye be in the right,
And do naething through the day
   That would gar them greet at night.

What fools are wilfu' bairns,
   Who misbehave frae hame!
There's something in the breast aye
   That tells them they're to blame;
And then when comes the gloamin',
   They're in a waefu' plight!
Sae do naething through the day
   That may gar ye greet at night.

Escape at Bedtime

The lights from the parlour and kitchen shone out
　Through the blinds and the windows and bars;
And high overhead and all moving about,
　There were thousands of millions of stars.
There ne'er were such thousands of leaves on a tree,
　Nor of people in church or the Park,
As the crowds of the stars that looked down upon me,
　And that glittered and winked in the dark.

The Dog, and the Plough, and the Hunter, and all,
　And the star of the sailor, and Mars,
These shone in the sky, and the pail by the wall
　Would be half full of water and stars.
They saw me at last, and they chased me with cries,
　And they soon had me packed into bed;
But the glory kept shining and bright in my eyes,
　And the stars going round in my head.

The Land of Counterpane

When I was sick and lay a-bed,
I had two pillows at my head,
And all my toys behind me lay
To keep me happy all the day.

And sometimes for an hour or so
I watched my leaden soldiers go,
With different uniforms and drills,
Among the bed-clothes, through the hills;

And sometimes sent my ships in fleets,
All up and down among the sheets;
Or brought my trees and houses out,
And planted cities all about.

I was the giant great and still
That sits upon the pillow-hill,
And sees before him, dale and plain,
The pleasant land of counterpane.

Young Night Thought

All night long and every night,
When my mamma puts out the light,
I see the people marching by,
As plain as day, before my eye.

Armies and emperors and kings,
And carrying different kinds of things,
And marching in so grand a way,
You never saw the like by day.

So fine a show was never seen
At the great circus on the green;
For every kind of beast and man
Is marching in that caravan.

At first they move a little slow,
But still the faster on they go,
And still beside them close I keep
Until we reach the town of sleep.

Of Such is the Kingdom of Heaven

Of such is the kingdom of heaven.
  No glory that ever was shed
From the crowning star of the seven
  That crown the north world's head,

No word that ever was spoken
  Of human or godlike tongue,
Gave ever such godlike token
  Since human harps were strung.

No sign that ever was given
  To faithful or faithless eyes
Showed ever beyond clouds riven
  So clear a Paradise.

Earth's creeds may be seventy times seven
  And blood have defiled each creed:
If of such be the kingdom of heaven,
  It must be heaven indeed.

The Salt of the Earth

If childhood were not in the world,
  But only men and women grown;
No baby-locks in tendrils curled,
  No baby-blossoms blown;

Though men were stronger, women fairer,
  And nearer all delights in reach,
And verse and music uttered rarer
  Tones of more godlike speech;

Though the utmost life of life's best hours
  Found, as it cannot now find, words;
Though desert sands were sweet as flowers
  And flowers could sing like birds;

But children never heard them, never
  They felt a child's foot leap and run,
This were drearier star than ever
  Yet looked upon the sun.

A Child's Laughter

All the bells of heaven may ring,
All the birds of heaven may sing,
All the wells on earth may spring,
All the winds on earth may bring
    All sweet sounds together;
Sweeter far than all things heard,
Hand of harper, tone of bird,
Sound of woods at sundown stirred,
Welling water's winsome word,
    Wind in warm wan weather,

One thing yet there is, that none
Hearing ere its chime be done
Knows not well the sweetest one
Heard of man beneath the sun,
    Hoped in heaven hereafter;
Soft and strong and loud and light,
Very sound of very light
Heard from morning's rosiest height,
When the soul of all delight
    Fills a child's clear laughter.

Golden bells of welcome rolled
Never forth such notes, nor told
Hours so blithe in tones so bold
As the radiant mouth of gold
    Here that rings forth heaven.
If the golden-crested wren
Were a nightingale – why, then,
Something seen and heard of men
Might be half as sweet as when
    Laughs a child of seven.

A Child's Pity

No sweeter thing than children's ways and wiles,
　　Surely, we say, can gladden eyes and ears;
Yet sometimes sweeter than their words or smiles
　　　Are even their tears.

To one for once a piteous tale was read,
　　How, when the murderous mother crocodile
Was slain, her fierce brood famished, and lay dead,
　　　Starved, by the Nile.

In vast green reed-beds on the vast grey slime
　　These monsters motionless and helpless lay,
Perishing only for the parent's crime
　　　Whose seed were they.

Hours after, toward the dusk, one blithe small bird
　　Of Paradise, who has our hearts in keeping,
Was heard or seen, but hardly seen or heard,
　　　For pity weeping.

He was so sorry, sitting still apart,
　　For the poor little crocodiles, he said.
Six years had given him, for an angel's heart,
　　　A child's instead.

Feigned tears the false beasts shed for murderous ends,
   We know from travellers' tales of crocodiles;
But these tears wept upon them of my friend's
    Outshine his smiles.

What heavenliest angels of what heavenly city
   Could match the heavenly heart in children here?
The heart that hallowing all things with its pity
    Casts out all fear?

So lovely, so divine, so dear their laughter
   Seems to us, we know not what could be more dear:
But lovelier yet we see the sign thereafter
    Of such a tear.

With sense of love half laughing and half weeping
   We met your tears, our small sweet-spirited friend:
Let your love have us in its heavenly keeping
    To life's last end.

Hymns for Infant Minds,

I. A Child's Hymn of Praise

I thank the goodness and the grace
   Which on my birth have smiled,
And made me, in these Christian days,
   A happy English child.

Sweet and Low

Sweet and low, sweet and low,
   Wind of the western sea,
Low, low, breathe and blow,
   Wind of the western sea!
Over the rolling waters go,
Come from the dying moon and blow,
   Blow him again to me;
While my little one, while my pretty one, sleeps.

Sleep and rest, sleep and rest,
   Father will come to thee soon;
Rest, rest on mother's breast,
   Father will come to thee soon;
Father will come to his babe in the nest,
Silver sails all out of the west
   Under the silver moon:
Sleep, my little one, sleep, my pretty one, sleep.

Letty's Globe

When Letty had scarce passed her third glad year,
　And her young, artless words began to flow,
One day we gave the child a coloured sphere
　Of the wide earth, that she might mark and know,
By tint and outline, all its sea and land.
　She patted all the world; old empires peeped
Between her baby fingers: her soft hand
　Was welcome at all frontiers. How she leaped,
And laughed, and prattled in her world-wide bliss;
　But when we turned her sweet unlearned eye
　On our own isle, she raised a joyous cry,
'Oh! yes. I see it. Letty's home is there!'
　And, while she hid all England with a kiss,
Bright over Europe fell her golden hair.

The Child on the Cliffs

Mother, the root of this little yellow flower
Among the stones has the taste of quinine.
Things are strange to-day on the cliff. The sun shines so bright,
And the grasshopper works at his sewing-machine
So hard. Here's one on my hand, mother, look;
I lie so still. There's one on your book.

But I have something to tell more strange. So leave
Your book to the grasshopper, mother dear,—
Like a green knight in a dazzling market-place—
And listen now. Can you hear what I hear
Far out? Now and then the foam there curls
And stretches a white arm out like a girl's.

Fishes and gulls ring no bells. There cannot be
A chapel or church between here and Devon,
With fishes or gulls ringing its bell,– hark!—
Somewhere under the sea or up in heaven.
'It's the bell, my son, out in the bay
On the buoy. It does sound sweet to-day.'

Sweeter I never heard, mother, no, not in all Wales.
I should like to be lying under that foam,
Dead, but able to hear the sound of the bell,
And certain that you would often come
And rest, listening happily.
I should be happy if that could be.

The Child in the Orchard

'He rolls in the orchard: he is stained with moss
And with earth, the solitary old white horse.
Where is his father and where is his mother
Among all the brown horses? Has he a brother?
I know the swallow, the hawk, and the hern;
But there are two million things for me to learn.

'Who was the lady that rode the white horse
With rings and bells to Banbury Cross?
Was there no other lady in England beside
That a nursery rhyme could take for a ride?

'Was there a man once who straddled across
The back of the Westbury White Horse
Over there on Salisbury Plain's green wall?
Was he bound for Westbury, or had he a fall?

'Out of all the white horses I know three,
At the age of six; and it seems to me
There is so much to learn, for men,
That I dare not go to bed again.
The swift, the swallow, the hawk, and the hern.
There are millions of things for me to learn.'

Snow

In the gloom of whiteness,
In the great silence of snow,
A child was sighing
And bitterly saying: 'Oh,
They have killed a white bird up there on her nest,
The down is fluttering from her breast!'
And still it fell through that dusky brightness
On the child crying for the bird of the snow.

Reinforcements

When little boys with merry noise
    In the meadows shout and run,
And little girls, sweet woman buds,
    Brightly open in the sun;—
I may not of the World despair,
    Whose God despaireth not, I see,
For blithesomer in Eden's air
    These lads and maidens could not be.

Why were they born, if Hope must die?
    Wherefore this health, if Truth should fail.
And why such Joy, if Misery
    Be conquering us and must prevail?
Arouse! Our spirit shall not droop:
    These young ones fresh from Heaven are;
Our God hath sent another troop
    And means to carry on the war.

The Retreat

Happy those early days, when I
Shined in my angel-infancy!
Before I understood this place
Appointed for my second race,
Or taught my soul to fancy ought
But a white, celestial thought;
When yet I had not walked above
A mile or two, from my first love,
And looking back – at that short space—
Could see a glimpse of His bright face;
When on some gilded cloud or flower,
My gazing soul would dwell an hour,
And in those weaker glories spy
Some shadows of eternity;
Before I taught my tongue to wound
My conscience with a sinful sound,
Or had the black art to dispense
A several sin to every sense,
But felt through all this fleshy dress
Bright shoots of everlastingness.
  O how I long to travel back
And tread again that ancient track!
That I might once more reach that plain
Where first I left my glorious train;
From whence the enlightened spirit sees
That shady City of palm trees!
But ah! my soul with too much stay
Is drunk, and staggers in the way!
Some men a forward motion love,
But I by backward steps would move;
And when this dust falls to the urn,
In that state I came, return.

On the Birthday of a Young Lady

Four Years Old

Old creeping time, with silent tread,
Has stol'n four years o'er Molly's head:
The rosebud opens on her cheek,
The meaning eyes begin to speak;
And in each smiling look is seen
The innocence which plays within.
Nor is the faltering tongue confined
To lisp the dawning of the mind,
But firm and full her words convey
The little all they have to say:
And each fond parent, as they fall,
Finds volumes in that little all.

　May every charm which now appears
Increase and brighten with her years!
And may that same old creeping time
Go on till she has reached her prime,
Then, like a master of his trade,
Stand still, nor hurt the work he made.

There was a Child went Forth

There was a child went forth every day,
And the first object he look'd upon, that object he became,
And that object became part of him for the day or a certain part
of the day,
Or for many years or stretching cycles of years.

The early lilacs became part of this child,
And grass and white and red morning-glories, and white and
red clover, and the song of the phœbe-bird,
And the Third-month lambs and the sow's pink-faint litter, and
the mare's foal and the cow's calf,
And the noisy brood of the barnyard or by the mire of the
pondside,
And the fish suspending themselves so curiously below there,
and the beautiful curious liquid,
And the water-plants with their graceful flat heads, all became
part of him.

The field-sprouts of Fourth-month and Fifth-month became part
of him,
Winter-grain sprouts and those of the light-yellow corn, and the
esculent roots of the garden,
And the apple-trees cover'd with blossoms and the fruit
afterward, and wood-berries, and the commonest weeds by
the road,
And the old drunkard staggering home from the outhouse of the
tavern whence he had lately risen,
And the schoolmistress that pass'd on her way to the school,
And the friendly boys that pass'd, and the quarrelsome boys,
And the tidy and fresh-cheek'd girls, and the barefoot negro boy
and girl,
And all the changes of city and country wherever he went.

His own parents, he that had father'd him and she that had
    conceiv'd him in her womb and birth'd him,
They gave this child more of themselves than that,
They gave him afterward every day, they became part of him.
The mother at home quietly placing the dishes on the supper-
    table,
The mother with mild words, clean her cap and gown, a
    wholesome odour falling off her person and clothes as she
    walks by,
The father, strong, self-sufficient, manly, mean, anger'd, unjust,
The blow, the quick loud word, the tight bargain, the crafty lure,
The family usages, the language, the company, the furniture,
    the yearning and swelling heart,
Affection that will not be gainsay'd, the sense of what is real,
    the thought if after all it should prove unreal,
The doubts of day-time and the doubts of night-time, the
    curious whether and how,
Whether that which appears so is so, or is it all flashes and
    specks?
Men and women crowding fast in the streets, if they are not
    flashes and specks what are they?
The streets themselves and the façades of houses, and goods in
    the windows,
Vehicles, teams, the heavy-plank'd wharves, the huge crossing
    at the ferries,
The village on the highland seen from afar at sunset, the river
    between,
Shadows, aureola and mist, the light falling on roofs and gables
    of white or brown two miles off,
The schooner near by sleepily dropping down the tide, the little
    boat slack-tow'd astern,
The hurrying tumbling waves, quick-broken crests, slapping,
The strata of colour'd clouds, the long bar of maroon-tint away
    solitary by itself, the spread of purity it lies motionless in,
The horizon's edge, the flying sea-crow, the fragrance of salt
    marsh and shore mud,
These became part of that child who went forth every day, and
    who now goes, and will always go forth every day.

A Child's Amaze

Silent and amazed even when a little boy,
I remember I heard the preacher every Sunday put God in his
  statements,
As contending against some being or influence.

In School-Days

Still sits the school-house by the road,
    A ragged beggar sunning;
Around it still the sumachs grow,
    And blackberry vines are running.

Within the master's desk is seen,
    Deep scarred by raps official;
The warping floor, the battered seats,
    The jack-knife's carved initial;

The charcoal frescoes on its wall;
    Its door's worn sill, betraying
The feet that, creeping slow to school,
    Went storming out to playing!

Long years ago a winter sun
    Shone over it at setting;
Lit up its western window-panes,
    And low eaves' icy fretting.

It touched the tangled golden curls,
    And brown eyes full of grieving,
Of one who still her steps delayed
    When all the school were leaving.

For near her stood the little boy
    Her childish favour singled;
His cap pulled low upon a face
    Where pride and shame were mingled.

Pushing with restless feet the snow
    To right and left, he lingered;—
As restlessly her tiny hands
    The blue-checked apron fingered.

He saw her lift her eyes; he felt
   The soft hand's light caressing,
And heard the tremble of her voice,
   As if a fault confessing.

'I'm sorry that I spelt the word:
   I hate to go above you,
Because,' – the brown eyes lower fell, –
   'Because, you see, I love you!'

Still memory to a grey-haired man
   That sweet child-face is showing.
Dear girl! the grasses on her grave
   Have forty years been growing!

He lives to learn in life's hard school,
   How few who pass above him
Lament their triumph and his loss,
   Like her, – because they love him.

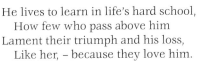

Boy at the Window

Seeing the snowman standing all alone
In dusk and cold is more than he can bear.
The small boy weeps to hear the wind prepare
A night of gnashings and enormous moan.
His tearful sight can hardly reach to where
The pale-faced figure with bitumen eyes
Returns him such a god-forsaken stare
As outcast Adam gave to Paradise.

The man of snow is, nonetheless, content,
Having no wish to go inside and die.
Still he is moved to see the youngster cry.
Though frozen, water is his element.
He melts enough to drop from one soft eye
A trickle of the purest rain, a tear
For the child at the bright pane, surrounded by
Such warmth, such light, such love, and so much fear.

To H. C.

Six Years Old

O Thou! whose fancies from afar are brought;
Who of thy words dost make a mock apparel,
And fittest to unutterable thought
The breeze-like motion and the self-born carol:
Thou faery voyager! that dost float
In such clear water, that thy boat
May rather seem
To brood on air than on an earthly stream;
Suspended in a stream as clear as sky,
Where earth and heaven do make one imagery;
O blessed vision! happy child!
Thou art so exquisitely wild,
I think of thee with many fears
For what may be thy lot in future years.
   I thought of times when Pain might be thy guest,
Lord of thy house and hospitality;
And Grief, uneasy lover! never rest
But when she sate within the touch of thee.
O too industrious folly!
O vain and causeless melancholy!
Nature will either end thee quite;
Or, lengthening out thy season of delight,
Preserve for thee, by individual right,
A young lamb's heart among the full-grown flocks.
What hast thou to do with sorrow,
Or the injuries of to-morrow?
Thou art a dew-drop, which the morn brings forth,
Ill fitted to sustain unkindly shocks,
Or to be trailed along the soiling earth;
A gem that glitters while it lives,
And no forewarning gives;
But, at the touch of wrong, without a strife
Slips in a moment out of life.

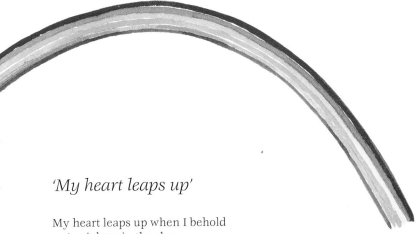

'My heart leaps up'

My heart leaps up when I behold
   A rainbow in the sky:
So was it when my life began;
So is it now I am a man;
So be it when I shall grow old,
   Or let me die!
The child is father of the Man;
And I could wish my days to be
Bound each to each by natural piety.

It is a beauteous evening, calm and free

It is a beauteous evening, calm and free,
The holy time is quiet as a Nun
Breathless with adoration; the broad sun
Is sinking down in its tranquillity;
The gentleness of heaven broods o'er the Sea:
Listen! the mighty Being is awake,
And doth with his eternal motion make
A sound like thunder – everlastingly.
Dear Child! dear Girl! that walkest with me here,
If thou appear untouched by solemn thought,
Thy nature is not therefore less divine:
Thou liest in Abraham's bosom all the year;
And worshipp'st at the Temple's inner shrine,
God being with thee when we know it not.

from '*The Prelude*'

There was a Boy

There was a Boy; ye knew him well, ye cliffs
And islands of Winander! – many a time,
At evening, when the earliest stars began
To move along the edges of the hills,
Rising or setting, would he stand alone,
Beneath the trees, or by the glimmering lake;
And there, with fingers interwoven, both hands
Pressed closely palm to palm and to his mouth
Uplifted, he, as through an instrument,
Blew mimic hootings to the silent owls,
That they might answer him. – And they would shout
Across the watery vale, and shout again,
Responsive to his call, – with quivering peals,
And long halloos, and screams, and echoes loud
Redoubled and redoubled; concourse wild
Of jocund din! And, when there came a pause
Of silence such as baffled his best skill:
Then, sometimes, in that silence, while he hung
Listening, a gentle shock of mild surprise
Has carried far into his heart the voice
Of mountain-torrents; or the visible scene
Would enter unawares into his mind
With all its solemn imagery, its rocks,
Its woods, and that uncertain heaven received
Into the bosom of the steady lake.

from ***Ode***

Intimations of Immortality from
Recollections of Early Childhood

The Child is father of the Man;
And I could wish my days to be
Bound each to each by natural piety.

I

There was a time when meadow, grove, and stream,
The earth, and every common sight,
        To me did seem
    Apparelled in celestial light,
The glory and the freshness of a dream:
It is not now as it hath been of yore—
    Turn whereso'er I may,
        By night or day,
The things which I have seen I now can see no more.

V

Our birth is but a sleep and a forgetting:
The Soul that rises with us, our life's Star,
    Hath had elsewhere its setting,
        And cometh from afar:
    Not in entire forgetfulness,
    And not in utter nakedness,
But trailing clouds of glory do we come
    From God, who is our home:
Heaven lies about us in our infancy!
Shades of the prison-house begin to close
    Upon the growing Boy
        But he

Beholds the light, and whence it flows,
    He sees it in his joy;
The Youth, who daily farther from the east
    Must travel, still is Nature's Priest,
    And by the vision splendid
    Is on his way attended;
At length the Man perceives it die away,
And fade into the light of common day.

VII

Behold the Child among his newborn blisses,
A six-years' Darling of a pygmy size!
See, where mid work of his own hand he lies,
Fretted by sallies of his mother's kisses,
With light upon him from his father's eyes!
See, at his feet, some little plan or chart,
Some fragment from his dream of human life,
Shaped by himself with newly-learnèd art;
    A wedding or a festival,
    A mourning or a funeral;
      And this hath now his heart,
    And unto this he frames his song;
      Then will he fit his tongue
To dialogues of business, love, or strife;
    But it will not be long
    Ere this be thrown aside,
    And with new joy and pride
The little Actor cons another part;
Filling from time to time his 'humorous stage'
With all the Persons, down to palsied Age,
That Life brings with her in her equipage;
    As if his whole vocation
    Were endless imitation.

~ *Index of first lines*

～ Acknowledgements

The editor and publishers wish to thank the following for permission to use copyright material:

Hilaire Belloc, for 'On the Gift of a Book to a Child'. Copyright © the Estate of Hilaire Belloc 1970, by permission of David Higham Associates on behalf of the Estate of the author; John Betjeman, for 'Summoned by Bells' from *Collected Poems* by John Betjeman, by permission of John Murray (Publishers) Ltd; Charles Causley, for 'Who?' from *Collected Poems* by Charles Causley, Macmillan, by permission of David Higham Associates on behalf of the author; Frances Cornford, for 'Childhood' from *Collected Poems* by Frances Cornford, by permission of the Trustees of the Frances Crofts Cornford Will Trust; Emily Dickinson, for 'How the waters closed above him' from *The Poems of Emily Dickinson*, edited by Thomas H. Johnson, The Belknap Press of Harvard University Press. Copyright © 1951, 1955, 1979 by the President and Fellows of Harvard College, by permission of the Trustees of Amherst College; Carol Ann Duffy, for 'In Mrs Tilscher's Class' from *The Other Country* (1990), by permission of Anvil Press Poetry Ltd; Harry Graham, for 'The Stern Parent' and 'Tender-Heartedness' from *Ruthless Rhymes* by Harry Graham, by permission of Laura Dance; Seamus Heaney, for 'Mid-Term Break' from *Opened Ground: Selected Poems 1966–1996* by Seamus Heaney. Copyright © 1998 by Seamus Heaney, by permission of Faber & Faber Ltd and Farrar Straus and Giroux LLC; A E Housman, for 'Infant Innocence', by permission of The Society of Authors as the Literary Representative of the Estate of the author; Ted Hughes, for 'Full Moon and Little Frieda' from *Birthday Letters* by Ted Hughes. Copyright © 1998 by Ted Hughes, by permission of Faber & Faber Ltd and Farrar Straus and Giroux LLC; Louis MacNeice, for 'Autobiography' from *Collected Poems* by Louis MacNeice, Faber and Faber, by permission of David Higham Associates on behalf of the author; Ogden Nash, for 'It is Indeed Spinach' from *Candy is Dandy: The Best of Ogden Nash*, Andre Deutsch. Copyright © 1938 by Ogden Nash, by permission of Carlton Books and Curtis Brown Ltd, New York, on behalf of the Estate of the author; Henry Newbolt, for 'Vitaï Lampada' from *Selected Poems of Henry Newbolt*, Hodder & Stoughton (1981), by permission of Peter Newbolt; Richard Wilbur, for 'Boy at the Window' from *New and Collected Poems* by Richard Wilbur, by permission of Faber & Faber Ltd.

Every effort has been made to trace the copyright holders but we have been unable to trace a number of poets, or their heirs. The publishers will be glad to hear from any such copyright holders.